Forget
That You Have Been
Hitler Soldiers

A Youth's Service to the Reich

By
Hermann O. Pfrengle
with
Wilbur D. Jones, Jr.

BURD STREET PRESS
SHIPPENSBURG, PENNSYLVANIA

This Burd Street Press publication
was printed by
Beidel Printing House, Inc.
63 West Burd Street
Shippensburg, PA 17257-0152 USA

The acid-free paper used in this book meets the guidelines for permanence and durability of the Committee on Production Guidelines for Book Longevity of the Council on Library Resources.

For a complete list of available publications
please write
Burd Street Press
Division of White Mane Publishing Company, Inc.
P.O. Box 152
Shippensburg, PA 17257-0152 USA

Library of Congress Cataloging-in-Publication Data

Pfrengle, Hermann O., 1929-
    Forget that you have been Hitler soldiers : a youth's service to the Reich / by Hermann O. Pfrengle with Wilbur D. Jones, Jr.
        p. cm.
    Includes bibliographical references and index.
    ISBN 1-57249-217-1 (alk. paper)
    1. Pfrengle, Hermann O., 1929- 2. World War,
1939-1945--Children--Germany--Biography. 3. World War, 1939-1945--Participation, Juvenile. 4. World War, 1939-1945--Personal narratives, German. 5.
Youth--Germany--Biography. 6. Deutsches Jungvolk (Organization)--Biography. I. Jones, Wilbur D., 1934- II. Title.

D811.5 .P48 2001
940.54'13'092--dc21
[B]
                                                                    2001025131

PRINTED IN THE UNITED STATES OF AMERICA

This memoir of World War II
is dedicated to the memory of my parents

Other Books by Wilbur D. Jones, Jr.

Hawaii Goes to War: The Aftermath of Pearl Harbor (with Carroll Robbins Jones)

Condemned to Live: A Panzer Artilleryman s Five-Front War (with Franz A. P. Frisch)

Gyrene: The World War II United States Marine

Giants in the Cornfield: The 27th Indiana Infantry

Arming the Eagle: A History of U.S. Weapons Acquisition Since 1775

Congressional Involvement and Relations: A Guide for Department of Defense Acquisition Managers, Four Editions

From Packard to Perry: A quarter Century of Service to the Defense Acquisition Community

Glossary: Defense Acquisition Acronyms and Terms, Two Editions

Visit his web site: *www.wilburjones.com*

Contents

Illustrations

Photos

Maps

Foreword

This book bears witness to a period in modern history which today's younger generations have not lived to see, and which gets oftentimes forgotten or memoratively pushed aside—for whatever reasons—by the older generations. Hermann Pfrengle's vividly told youth memoir, with World War II as its central experience, opens up new perspectives in the historical view and interpretation of that period, and represents a much welcomed break with stereotyped perceptions, and myths, about those times. It provokes in-depth thought about the cataclysmic event of World War II, its causes, effects, and the realization how lastingly our conception of today's world has been preshaped by it.

From my own experience as a *Jungvolk* cub of about the same age as Hermann Pfrengle, I can spontaneously empathize with much of his story, as seen through the eyes of a *Jungvolk* member. It makes me recall my own mandatory membership in the *Jungvolk*, its originally romanticized boy scout ideals, ethnically garnished by the National Socialists, and the shrewd methods attempted by *Jungvolk* leaders to incite in our barely 10-year-old minds and hearts some enthusiasm for the Nazi system. But having had to witness with immense shock how, on November 9, 1938, SS and SA members set afire and destroyed the Jewish synagogue located near my parental home in Bonn, I just couldn't muster the enthusiasm those youth leaders expected of me.

Indisputably, the National Socialist ideology succeeded in misleading the German youths of the time. From today's perspective, the process involved is easier to understand if one keeps in mind that National Socialism's guiding idea of youth education was the mythical concept of "Struggle, Blood and Honor," reflected by propaganda against the historical background of the Fatherland's periods of greatness and demeanor, the latter exemplified by the Treaty of Versailles and its disastrous consequences for Germany and its population. The continuous propagandist reminder of those who had given their lives in World War I, and later in the Nazis' political struggle, served the purpose of creating a deep belief in a Germany embroiled in National Socialism, to live in this belief, and also to die for it. Ultimately, some of the highest leaders in the Reich's organizations sacrificed, by orders of Hitler and his henchmen, their people's youth to the phantom idea that the Fatherland ranked higher in value than individual death.

Psychologically speaking, National Socialism, as an all-encompassing movement, effected the growth of a pathological mix of genuine patriotic love with nationalism peaking in brutality, of justified ethnic self-confidence with an indoctrinated racial superiority complex, and of a naive desire to believe with fatal self-delusion. Most Germans—and, above all, of course, the youth—realized too late that Hitler's National Socialist megalomania would ultimately lead to the Fatherland's demise.

World War I may be characterized as the first major international conflict with political-ideological traits, as reflected, for example, in the U.S. President Woodrow Wilson's intention "to make the world safe for democracy." World War II was clearly an ideological conflict of contending ideologies and their universal missions of Fascism, National Socialism, Soviet Communism, and Western democracy-based capitalism, and with both political-ideological principles and power at stake.

The sheer military power potentials in World War II as they relate to Germany and the United States in the European theater are comprehensively presented by Wilbur Jones. Another important part of this book's introduction deals with the development and structure of National Socialist organizations.

While World War I was the "war to end war," the victors of World War II spoke even more emphatically about the "need to build a better world." When the fledgling Federal Republic of Germany, after six years of extremely arduous reconstruction efforts, had become part of this better world, my German government career path coincided with that of Hermann Pfrengle. In the course of our joint German government service, I have come to hold his meritorious work dedicated to Germany's security and economic prosperity within the western alliance in the highest esteem. The same goes for his invaluable advice based on his internationally recognized professional expertise and many years of U.S. experience. As one of his former superiors sharing his age group, I am proud to say that the bond between us is deeper than can be expressed in this foreword.

It may be relatively easy to impute "inevitability" to historical processes. This can be a tempting substitute for deeper investigation and critical thought. The fact that such an expedient way out was not chosen in this book enhances its contemporary historical value. Last, but not least, while there are many war books about fighting on "out-of-country" fronts, only a few deal with personal experiences on the German home front. I am confident the informed reader will find Hermann Pfrengle's youth memoir both knowledge-enhancing and thought-provoking.

Hans J. Dohmgoergen
Principal Councillor
Ministry of Defense (Retired)
Federal Republic of Germany
Raubling, Germany

Preface

In the mid-1990s I was working with Dr. Franz A. P. Frisch to write his memoir of World War II service as a nine-year German soldier. We sold an excerpt outlining primarily his experiences in the 1941 campaign in the Soviet Union to *World War II* magazine, which published the article, "A Panzer Soldier's War," in the September 1995 issue.

The article and ensuing conversations attracted the attention of Hermann O. Pfrengle, a German national and a long-time Washington representative of the Ministry of Defense of the Federal Republic of Germany (FRG). He and Frisch had met for the first time in 1978 at the U.S. Department of Defense Systems Management College (DSMC), at Fort Belvoir, Virginia, an institution educating military and civilian personnel in the defense systems acquisition business. Frisch was on the faculty, and later became a professor emeritus. H. Pfrengle began guest lecturing on West German, North Atlantic Treaty Organization (NATO), and multinational program management. Subsequently, DSMC honored H. Pfrengle as an Honorary International Professor, the college's second-only such designation.

Frisch and I later served together as DSMC professors for 10 years. He introduced me to his friend H. Pfrengle over lunch in 1994. We asked for H. Pfrengle's help in obtaining contacts at official German documentation centers and archives, and he readily agreed to do so. H. Pfrengle suggested he and I work together to develop and write his own remembrances of war service as a member of the younger boys' class of the Hitler Youth, the *Jungvolk*, for inclusion in the Frisch book. It would contrast his home-front experiences with Frisch's as a front-line soldier. Frisch agreed. Easily I concluded that H. Pfrengle's story was of immense historical value and had to be told, particularly as interest in World War II history was at its peak in the United States, and we began working together on this project. The original proposal to White Mane was to include both memoirs in the same book, but White Mane ultimately decided to publish the two memoirs separately. The Frisch memoir, *Condemned to Live: A Panzer Artilleryman s Five-Front War,* was released in early 2000.[1]

H. Pfrengle at age nine became a member of the *Jungvolk.* He grew up on the home front along the Rhine River amidst Allied air raids, worked for months building the *Westwall* (Siegfried Line), at 15 was pressed into active paramilitary service in the war's final weeks, was captured by the Americans after retreating from the Rhine into Czechoslovakia, and spent an incredible odyssey returning home through a defeated and devastated Germany.

H. Pfrengle began researching and drafting his memoir, focusing on his activities in the *Jungvolk* at home and on the front lines, and the retreat from the Rhine before the advancing Americans in the spring of 1945. He described his family, childhood, school days, and captivity. His material came from personal recollections, limited family records, publications, and official and unofficial documents. In collaborating with him, I researched appropriate subjects such as the *Jungvolk* and Hitler Youth movement and the U.S. Army's campaign in western, central, and southeastern Germany, from February to the European war's end on May 8, 1945, coedited his manuscript, and obtained a publishing contract with White Mane.

We drew from his detailed memory and selected photographs and illustrations. He ably supplements his remembrances of situations with first-hand accounts he translated from numerous German sources and checking with personal sources in Germany and the United States. (One of his Washington responsibilities to the FRG government was utilizing his total fluency in English to translate for President George Bush and Chancellor Helmut Kohl in international conferences.)

The 15-year-old H. Pfrengle, by "election" of his peers, while retreating, found himself responsible for his group of hometown youngsters seeking first to avoid, then to contact, the Americans, and later to lead them home. H. Pfrengle was called into active service in March 1945 at the time Germany was collapsing militarily. In spite of his compulsory role in having built fortifications at the Siegfried Line, and acting as messenger, observer, and scout for distraught *Wehrmacht* units, he essentially was in no position to be of much value to his country's defensive effort. His memoir ends following his two-month return home by foot and rail, and afterthoughts.

The book's title, *Forget That You Have Been Hitler Soldiers*, was the admonition of the American army officer who released H. Pfrengle and his comrades from a prisoner of war camp in late May 1945, in Tittling, Germany. With the wave of a hand the boys were dispatched homeward almost all the way westward across Germany with little but the shirts on their backs.

His noteworthy recall of details is illuminating and greatly embellishes his story. He reports on and adds a valuable contribution to an aspect of the war from the German side to which history has paid inadequate attention in English-language literature: the life, culture, travails, and service on the home front and at the front lines by boys who served the Third Reich. The reader is thrust into:

Accounts of wartime home life as a student and member of the *Jungvolk*;

Both invigoration and desperation in building the "invincible" Siegfried Line;

Chilling remembrances of the role of *Waffen*-SS troops in policing (and assassinating) those among the military, *Volkssturm*, *Jungvolk*, and Hitler Youth units, and the civilians, who would surrender, desert, or openly defy SS orders;

Relationships with his *Jungvolk* comrades and with members of the *Wehrmacht, Volkssturm*, and older Hitler Youth;

The personal fears, instincts, flexibility, and adjustment to being in combat, and near an enemy whose machines and guns he could always hear, whose fire he survived with some close calls, but whose soldiers he seldom saw in person;

The picture of German soldiers and civilians surviving air raids and shelling, enduring severe shortages of food and other basics of life;

The cities, towns, villages, rivers, forests, and mountain ranges—
the route—through which he trekked from March 16 to May
6, 1945, before being captured, and his involvement in combat;
The utter frustration, demoralization, and disorganization of
German military units in the closing weeks, including the ill-
fated "Schoerner's last stand" attack ordered by Hitler of
which H. Pfrengle was to be a part; and
Accounts of the indiscriminate bombing and shelling of German towns and residences, and indignities he and other German prisoners of war endured in the first weeks after the war
ended—which might cause Americans to wince.

H. Pfrengle used numerous supplementary reference sources
including the Babenhausen, Germany, city archives; Guenter Sagan,
[article translation] "The Destruction of Hauswurz in 1945," in
Fuldaer Zeitung, February 21, 1996; Generalmajor Oskar Munzel,
MGFA, No. B-360 [report translation] "Tank Training Combat
Command Thuringia, 27 March to 5 April, 1945"; Adolf Hossfeld,
[article translation] "The Collapse in April 1945 in Sonneberg," in
Neue Presse, January 30, 1993; Helmut Ritgen, [article translation]
"The Demand that Dragged the War on," in *Statesman*, New Delhi,
June 18, 1995; Michael Fischl, ed. [book translation] *The Ameri-
cans are Coming* (Tittling, Germany: Verlag Herbert Dorfmeister,
1995); [book translation] *Bitter Times* (Pressath, Germany: Eckard
Bodner Publishers, 1995); and Percy E. Schramm, ed. [book trans-
lation] *War Diary of the* Wehrmacht *s Supreme Command* (Frank-
furt/Main, Germany, 1965).

With retirement in 1994, H. Pfrengle completed a long and con-
structive service to his country in the fields of international political, technological, and defense cooperation, much of the time spent
in the United States. Widely respected and appreciated in these fields
throughout the NATO community and beyond, his involvement continues from his Herndon, Virginia, home.

Wilbur D. Jones, Jr.
Wilmington, North Carolina

Prologue

The grim landmark of World War II is probably the 20th century's sharpest divide between present and future generations. Too young to be inducted into the German *Wehrmacht*, but not too young to be forced into Hitler's last desperate effort to "save the Fatherland," I rather straddled this generational divide, and my memoir of those cataclysmic times reflects aspects from both sides of it.

Many of these memories are still vividly present in my mind; others lay buried under the rubble of history, or had become subject to the soothing process of psychological displacement. The older one gets, the more one tends to look back at his own life, and I was no exception to this popular wisdom as, after my 1994 retirement in the United States from the Federal Republic of Germany's government service, I began to play with the idea of sharing my wartime experiences with others.

The main motivation for writing my memoir was to tell, to the best of my memory and with the help of documentary evidence, my personal account of growing up in the Third Reich, and participating in its final collapse as a 15-year-old conscript. It is a story in the sense of "lessons learned." I sincerely hope the reader will reflect on the dangers of perverted ideology, misled idealism, and excessive nationalism which, as history continues to demonstrate, are by no means limited to the Nazi regime.

I also wish to invite the reader's attention to the way in which the European war turned out to be basically different from preceding wars. Previously in modern times, a state's defenses had been

its frontiers or front lines. Its
armies acted as a carapace that
short of disaster sheltered its civilians—and many of its generals—in the rear. In World War
II, with massive air attacks and
ultimate all-out conscription (in
Germany, from boys as young as
13 years to old men of 65), the
distinction between military and
civilian targets and victims was
virtually indistinguishable and
unobserved (a process carried to
the ultimate extreme in extermi-
nation camps). The civilian
population immediately found
itself as part of the front lines.

H. Pfrengle as a *Jungvolk* leader, 1943

More issues exist of genera-
tion-spanning concern: for example, the dubious concept of "unconditional surrender." I am sure that a few of the Allies, one of the
possible exceptions being U.S. Secretary of the Treasury Henry
Morgenthau, Jr., and his ill-conceived plan for the de-industrialized
Germany, had fully realized the implications of their demand for
Germany's unconditional capitulation. Understandable as this concept might have been in response to Hitler's waging of "total war," it
was bound to prolong the conflict; but this is not all. Demanding the
surrender not just of the regime, but of a nation, this concept helped
create a divisive political void in the wasteland that was then the
heart of Europe. Only in a Machiavellian sense can "unconditional
surrender" be interpreted as a corollary to Hitler's "total war."

In addressing the American political principle of strict separation between church and state, I focus on the attitude of a high-
ranking German army chaplain, contrasting it with the charitable
deeds traditional institutions of the Catholic Church afforded me
and my Protestant comrades when no one else was there to assist.

Finally, there is the somber realization that it is much easier to
start a war than to end one. The Nazis kept on fighting to Germany's
total collapse and Allied conquest, and though hostilities ended on

May 8, 1945, World War II continued against Germany until the Western Allies declared it ended, without a formal peace treaty, in 1951. While there may be nothing in human nature that makes war inevitable, there isn't anything in it that would assure peace as a permanent state of the world, either. History shows that war to make peace can spawn another war. Men will continue to be wrong and worse, do wrong. In my humble opinion, the problem of controlling war may perhaps be considered more promisingly not as action to realize a plan, but as a continuous process of adjustment and democratization to achieve and maintain stability in a complex world.

This memoir is my personal story as seen through a youngster's eyes brutally opened by his war experiences. As such, it is, of course, subjective, and was not written with the idea of a history textbook in mind.

The book's preface and introduction are essentially of Wilbur D. Jones, Jr.'s making and reflect primarily his views as a military historian. He also was my book agent who, to use his own words, did his "level best" to coedit and process the manuscript for printing. I appreciate his energetic commitment, particularly in the book's early proof stage, to get the job done.

I thank Herbert Dorfmeister Publishers of Tittling, Germany, and that town's mayor, Anton Zauhar, for making available materials and documents related to the war's last weeks and my captivity in eastern Bavaria. Mayor Wolfgang Kohn of Mettlach, Germany, deserves my gratitude for letting me use photographs associated with my stint on the Siegfried Line. I am also indebted to numerous other German sources for their generous assistance.

At the Defense Systems Management College, a congenial atmosphere of international understanding provided me with opportunities to associate academically both with the faculty's specialist and interdisciplinary minds. I am thankful for the intellectual stimulation of my work on this book. This collegial environment was particularly fostered by professors Franz Frisch, Richard Kwatnoski, R. Don Hood, and Christopher Scott. I acknowledge with gratitude their valuable advice, support, and outstanding cooperation, also in matters reaching beyond the immediate scope of this book.

Hermann O. Pfrengle
Herndon, Virginia

Introduction

The Land Campaigns in Europe

World War II began on September 1, 1939, when the German armed forces, the *Wehrmacht*, invaded next door neighbor Poland. It ended in Europe on May 8, 1945, when Germany surrendered to the Allies, her armies totally defeated on its eastern and western fronts, and much of her Fatherland destroyed or desolated. The most cataclysmic event in the 20th century, World War II, including the conflicts in Asia, the Pacific, Atlantic, Mediterranean, and other theaters, killed approximately 60,000,000 people, military and civilians, and left countless millions wounded, missing, or uprooted and homeless. The human suffering was immeasurable, the national treasury of most participating nations drained or extended to the utmost.

To orient the reader about the European land war and its major events and organizations affecting Hermann O. Pfrengle's association with the *Jungvolk,* Hitler Youth, and *Volkssturm,* the authors provide a brief overview.

Adolf Hitler was directly responsible for World War II. An Austrian by birth but ardent German nationalist, he had joined the Nazi Party in the early 1920s. Once he took over the party leadership in 1923, the Nazi name would eventually become synonymous with the scourge of most of Europe and the world. Hitler's rise to power was born out of three compelling reasons: (1) Germany's quest to rebuild its economy after its collapse from the Treaty of Versailles, which culminated Germany's defeat in World War I, and in the Great Depression; (2) revenge for losing the war to its "natural" enemies

France and Britain; and (3) loathing of the communist Soviet Union. Hitler charmed the German people at the beginning by showing them a way out of their economic and national demise. The armed forces became the principal means of accomplishing his goals, and he devoted significant national attention and resources into rebuilding its numbers and stature.

On January 30, 1933, the opportunistic Hitler was appointed German chancellor by the aging Reich president and former army field marshal Paul von Hindenburg, having never been elected by the German people to any post. Fate played into Hitler's hands when Hindenburg died on August 2, 1934. He forced the merging of the chancellorship and presidency, which gave him supreme command of the armed forces, and soldiers took an oath of allegiance to him personally. He then had a free hand as dictator, or *Fuehrer*.

Veiled under Hitler's slogan of "Work and Peace" was the intention to wage war to attain his objectives, and in 1936 he ordered a plan for having the armed forces and the economy ready for war in four years. He believed war with the U.S.S.R. was inevitable, particularly to accommodate his long-standing dream of more *Lebensraum* (living space) for the German population, defeating Bolshevism and gaining access to Soviet oil fields. His first overt military act was to reoccupy in 1936 the Rhineland, the heavily industrialized western area of Germany taken away by the Allies after World War I.

In March 1938, he took advantage of political unrest in Austria and annexed that country, with the apparent consent of its people, in the Anschluss, or joining up of his home country with the Third Reich. One year later, he sent troops into Czechoslovakia's Sudetenland, the German-leaning area across its border, and until 1918 part of Austria, to seize that territory. No one stopped him from these actions short of outcries and resolutions which he ignored. He was on his way to near total domination of the continent by 1942. Meanwhile, the scheming and relentless Hitler protected against Russian intervention on the east by signing a non-aggression treaty with the Soviet Union, one he would tear up in June 1941 when the time came for him also to execute his long-term goal, conquering that nation and defeating Bolshevism.

To counter Polish persecution of some Germans who had remained in that part of western Poland which had been German territory until the 1919 Treaty of Versailles, Hitler staged an event on the Polish border used as a pretense for authorizing the immediate pre-planned attack on Poland on September 1, 1939. The *Wehrmacht* streaked into and across Poland, employing a revolutionary type of warfare called *Blitzkrieg*, which utilized the Panzers—tanks and armored infantry—supported by attack aircraft and motorized artillery, to thrust fast and deep into enemy territory, and surround isolated pockets of troops. By September 27, the first nation to surrender to Germany had fallen. Germany's principal western antagonists, France, and to a lesser degree Great Britain, along with Australia and New Zealand, declared war on Germany two days after the invasion of Poland. As one of the Axis powers, Germany declared war on the United States on December 11, 1941, after the U.S. had declared war on Axis ally Japan on December 8.

Europe then settled into what western historians call the "Phoney War," while the world watched for Hitler's next move. On April 9, 1940, Hitler preempted a British invasion of independent Norway by three days and invaded the country himself after the British began mining Norwegian waters, intercepting ore shipments to Germany, and engaging the Germans at sea with mutual losses. German forces occupied independent Denmark on April 10, and Norway fell on June 10 after beaten British and French forces withdrew and the Norwegians were overcome. The German campaign in Norway was a strategic textbook operation of the highest order and included history's first airborne drop.

On May 10, Hitler launched the long-anticipated invasion of France, Luxembourg, Belgium, and the Netherlands. Five days later the Netherlands capitulated, and on the 28th, Belgium. German Panzers reached the Calais coast and Dunkirk on the 26th, and despite having trapped hundreds of thousands of Allied troops on the English Channel beaches, were halted by Hitler, allowing most of them to escape to England.[1] By June 14, Germans entered Paris, and on the 25th, a cease-fire ended the Battle of France.

Hitler's momentous decision to take his war to the Soviet Union precipitated the largest invasion of the war, Operation *Barbarossa*, and its bloodiest and fiercest prolonged campaign. Beginning on June 22, 1941, some 3.6 million German and other Axis soldiers (including Hungarians and Rumanians, and assisted by Finland and Bulgaria) with 3,600 tanks and more than 2,700 aircraft, crossed the border with the U.S.S.R. through the partitioned Poland. For the opening weeks it was *Blitzkrieg* again at its finest. But soon the drive began to peter out because of overextended logistics lines, command and communications problems, bad weather, and eventually the harsh Russian winter. In late November the Panzers reached the outskirts of Moscow, one of Hitler's strategic objectives, but no further. Fierce Soviet counterattacks, and the extreme cold, for which the invaders had no winter clothing, combined to push the Germans back in December. In 1942 the Soviets gained the offensive and began forcing their enemy westward. German drives southward into Ukraine and the Caucasus, with Hitler's objective of the Baku oil fields in mind, ended in disaster at Stalingrad in February 1943 and at Kursk in July. From then on, the German advances turned into total retreat along the Eastern Front until the fall of Berlin in May 1945.

In 1943, as the German-Italian North African campaign collapsed, and the Mediterranean war spread closer to Europe, German forces began augmenting Axis partner Italy in Sicily. British and American forces landed in Sicily on July 10, 1943, and quickly swept aside the defenders, entering the objective Messina on August 17. With Sicily taken, the Germans and Italians escaped to the boot of Italy to prepare for the inevitable Allied landings. Italy surrendered on September 3. On September 9 the Allies came ashore at Salerno and Reggio Calabria. The arduous 20-month campaign up the Italian peninsula, the Germans continuously on the defensive behind well-fortified positions, ended on May 2, 1945, in the northern Po River Valley. There the routed German forces, retreating hurriedly northward, surrendered.

Following the Allied landings in France at Normandy in June 1944, Paris was liberated on August 25, and the drive through France and Belgium toward Germany continued into November when a stalemate developed. In December, Hitler launched Germany's final massive assault of the war into the Ardennes Forest, attempting to drive the Allies back to the Channel. It failed in the Battle of the Bulge, and the Allies capitalized by defeating the *Westwall* (Siegfried Line)[2] inside the German border as 1945 began and advanced on the Rhine River. The Americans first crossed the Rhine, Germany's last natural defensive barrier on the Western Front, at Remagen on March 7, and other crossings soon followed. By late March, the

Allies were ready for their final campaign into central and southern Germany.

As the Americans pushed forward from the area of Mainz and Frankfurt, the Germans were reduced to uncoordinated and ill-prepared defensive efforts while retreating inward. Allied drives moved southward and eastward into Bavaria, Austria, and Czechoslovakia, until by late April few organized German units of size remained. Thwarting the American drive from the Rhine at Mainz into Czechoslovakia was the task of the disorganized and ill-supplied army units to which H. Pfrengle was loosely attached and swept along. These were his seven weeks of combat service to the Reich before the American forces under Lieutenant General George S. Patton, Jr., captured him near Vimperk, Czechoslovakia, on May 6.

Meanwhile, the Soviets were rapidly moving westward toward Berlin and helped create a viselike grip on the enveloped enemy. On April 30 Hitler committed suicide in Berlin. Germany surrendered on May 8, called VE-(Victory in Europe) Day, and the European War ended.

The *Wehrmacht*

In 1938, Hitler established the *Oberkommando der Wehrmacht* (*OKW, Wehrmacht* High Command) as the armed forces machinery for executing the coming war. He retained the title as supreme commander and named army Field Marshal Wilhelm Keitel as *Wehrmacht* chief of staff and army Field Marshal Alfred Jodl as chief of operations. Both remained for the duration of the war.

The *Wehrmacht* consisted of the three services, the army (*Heer,* the army command was the *OKH, Oberkommando des Heeres*), navy (*Kriegsmarine*), and air force (*Luftwaffe,* including *Flak*), each seeking to preserve its vested interests. Each service commander had direct access to Hitler, making overall strategic coordination difficult. At their peaks, the army mustered 6.55 million men in 1943, the navy 801,000 in 1944, and the air force 1.0 million in 1942. The *Waffen*-SS, directed by the SS and only loosely associated with the *Wehrmacht*, peaked at 830,000 in 1945.

This is not surprising, as after the failed attempt on Hitler's life by army officers on July 20, 1944, he no longer trusted the army and assigned control of the *Heimatheer* (army units stationed on German soil) and the *Volkssturm* to SS chief Heinrich Himmler. That provided

Himmler with a free hand to recruit more personnel into the *Waffen-SS*, including from territories with some German ethnicity. For the entire military, the peak was 9.48 million in 1943, twice its number when war began. *Wehrmacht* losses in killed in action were: army, 1,622,561; navy, 48,904; air force 138,596, for a total of 1,810,061. The total who died from other causes was 191,338. Wounded included: army, 4,145,863; navy, 25,259; air force 216,579. The total missing was 1,902,704.[3]

In 1939, the army consisted of the following number of divisions (total 106): six Panzer, four motorized (later Panzer Grenadier, or armored infantry), four light armored, 86 infantry, and a few others. By 1945, the principal division numbers had become (total 304, in varying degrees of strength): 31 Panzer, 13 motorized, 176 infantry, and 50 *Volksgrenadier*. True to Hitler's in-house policy of "divide and rule," to enhance his maintaining detailed direct control over the *Wehrmacht*, the air force had the parachute forces, some field divisions, a Panzer division, and the anti-aircraft *(Flak)* forces. And of course there was the SS and *Waffen*-SS, which often operated without army control but in their areas. Conflicts arose over the chain of command. After June 1941, the Eastern Front became Germany's primary theater where 60 percent of the army forces were involved.

As the strong possibility of defeat faced Germany in 1944, Hitler in September created the *Volkssturm* (People's Home Defense Force) organization, making men ages 16–60 (some younger, some older) liable for civil defense service at the home front. The *Volkssturm* did not fall under the *Wehrmacht* but came under the loose control of Himmler.[4] Because the men were also part of the civilian labor force, training was accomplished on weekends. Arms and ammunition were scarce, and men wore their own civilian clothes with arm bands identifying them as *Volkssturm*. By 1945, the *Volkssturm* was deployed in the front lines, sometimes assimilating Hitler Youth and *Jungvolk* groups to fight alongside. But their fighting contributions were generally negligible.

In the 1930s, inspired by General Heinz Guderian, the Germans formed armored (Panzer) divisions for all phases of land warfare. Guderian led Panzer forces into Poland, France, and Russia, and later was *OKH* chief of staff. Panzer divisions ideally consisted

of tanks, armored cars, mechanized (motorized) infantry, motorized artillery, and motorized engineers. Deployment of these armored
units in *Blitzkrieg* attacks was the foundation of German army tactics until 1943 when they lost the initiative (except for the Ardennes
offensive in December 1944), although most troops either walked or
utilized horses for transportation.

The *Hitlerjugend* and the *Jungvolk*

The *Hitlerjugend* (Hitler Youth) began in 1926 as a Nazi organization for young men 14 to 18. In 1929 it absorbed the girls' equivalent, *Bund Deutscher Maedel* (Federation of German Maidens). In
1931, it absorbed some of the 10–14 age groups, including the boys'
Deutsches Jungvolk (German Young People) and the girls'
Jungmaedelbund (Young Maidens' Federation). Membership grew
from 2.3 million in 1933, when it became a state organization with
Hitler's assumption of power, to 7.7 million by 1939. In 1940 membership was made compulsory. The *Jungvolk* existed in various forms
and organizations from the early 1900s to promote German values,
customs, and love of home and the people.

For Hermann O. Pfrengle, joining the *Jungvolk* in April 1939
was a joyous initiation occasion. At long last he could be part of an
officially recognized, organized, and uniformed youth group which
even the grownups seemed to respect. During his first two years of
membership he enjoyed the regular weekly meetings filled with activities that captured a boy's interest and imagination, and hikes,
camps, and local sports competitions.

Regarding the initiation rite, a brief and rather unceremonious
act, he was unaware of any political indoctrination or intent. He
was too young to understand the meaning of such concepts, and the
environment he was being raised in was the only one he knew and,
therefore, he perceived it as righteous. H. Pfrengle and his young
associates had to promise before the local *Jungvolk* top leader
(*Faehnleinfuehrer*, about 16 or 17 years old) to be tough, faithful,
good comrades, and to uphold honor, the highest of all values. He
does not remember ever having sworn to an oath about "helping the
Fuehrer (Hitler)," and "so help me God." (At least one author, H. W.
Koch, describing the Hitler Youth movement stated that such an oath
was standard at induction in "the Marienburg, the ancient capital of
the Teutonic order...new member of the *Jungvolk* swore the oath that

was to be repeated every 20 April....")[5] Marienburg was in East Prussia which, from 1919 until the end of Hitler's 1939 campaign in Poland, was a German enclave surrounded by Polish and Lithuanian territory and the Baltic Sea, with unhindered access from Germany by sea only. H. Pfrengle is certain that it would have been virtually impossible to transport more than a million new members annually to Marienburg for such rites, and thinks that perhaps a select few were given this opportunity. He cannot recall meeting any boys who had ever been there, and refuses to accept a view that "in Nazi Germany childhood ceased at the age of ten; thereafter, there were only 'political soldiers' of the future."[6] And from his experience, membership in the Hitler Youth as a rule was followed by one or two years of service in the *Reichsarbeitdienst* (Reich Labor Service). Koch does not mention this organization.[7] (This is surprising because more than a million young German men must have been inducted into this service over a period of several years.)

German youth organizations from 1933–45 were not as monolithic as the Reich Youth Leadership would have wished to make them. There were general differences between the *Jungvolk* and the Hitler Youth, such as in their pledges, uniforms, organizational designations, and content of duties. Some local groups also continued pre-Nazi traditions from Boy Scouts, patriotic, religious, and sports movements. Only the professional (i.e., Nazi-instituted and paid leadership corps of the Hitler Youth) on up was ideologically unified, and even at that level, significant differences existed. Also, regional differences regarding titles and functions of youth leaders, including in the *Jungvolk*, make it difficult to display any kind of standard organizational tables.[8] For example, *Jungvolk* in the Mainz region where H. Pfrengle was raised did not know the rank of *Unterbannfuehrer*. It was not a standard designation. The Mainz region instead had a *Jungstammfuehrer* in charge of about six hundred boys, a rank not recognized throughout the movement. H. Pfrengle's 1944 *Jungvolk* rank of *Hauptjungzugfuehrer*, number two in charge of about 150 boys, ranked between the number one, *Faehnleinfuehrer*, and *Jungzugfuehrer*, in charge of about 30-40. But his rank does not appear in either of two organizational charts studied.[9]

At least in the Mainz region, *Jungvolk* leaders who had risen through the ranks, such as H. Pfrengle, remained with their *Jungvolk* groups and did not become members of the Hitler Youth (generally the organization of the 14–18 year olds). If there were standard *Jungvolk* nationwide organizational structures, they were either not totally adopted or were modified by the higher leaders in the Mainz region, and possibly elsewhere.

Long before Hitler came to power, the German *Jungvolk,* existing in various forms and groups, promoted German values, customs, and love of home, nature, and the German people. By 1930, some of the *Jungvolk* leadership identified with others in disputing that Germany was solely responsible for World War I, and opposing the Versailles Treaty and Young Plan. It was a matter of time before those leaders would with other vocals loudly proclaim such patriotic and nationalistic catchwords associated with the Nazis. The German *Jungvolk* was not the only youth movement with German-Austrian roots that relinquished, under Nazi pressure, political and ideological independence to permit absorption by the Hitler Youth. For example, the Boy Scouts Federation of Austria joined the Austrian Hitler Youth before the 1938 Anschluss.

Four German states in 1932 prohibited membership in the *Jungvolk* to prevent political indoctrination of school children. For a brief period that year, all Nazi organizations were legally banned in Germany, including the *Jungvolk* and Hitler Youth. Because some of the *Jungvolk* groups voluntarily subordinated themselves to the Hitler Youth,[10] it became their parade horse vis-à-vis other youth movements. It demonstrated that traditional and romanticized values, including love of nature, home, singing songs around the campfire, and sports, could be retained under the Hitler Youth umbrella. Throughout its existence the *Jungvolk* retained many elements of its various pre-World War I groups' structures, for example, a *Horde* of about 6 boys; a *Jungenschaft* of about 12, and a *Faehnlein* of about 120–150.

Although there was no ideologically homogeneous Hitler Youth leadership, the social strata of the Hitler Youth and *Jungvolk* provides a better indicator of homogeneity. Compulsory membership injected a middle-class flavor, and by 1939 this class dominated membership in both groups. Only when it came to combat service did any distinction between the Hitler Youth and *Jungvolk* cease. Even 11 year olds could carry and fire the *Panzerfaust* recoilless antitank grenade launcher. Girls manned *Flak* anti-aircraft guns. Youthful fanaticism at the front was the exception rather than the rule, but there were cases of Hitler Youth ambushes and artillery action against U.S. infantry where they sometimes fought to the last boy.

The ideological and indoctrination base for such fanaticism varied regionally and locally and depended upon many factors. As a secondary school student, H. Pfrengle originally was earmarked to be drafted into service as a *Flakhelfer*. The official Nazi decree on this type of service read, "These boys shall be assigned only duties which correspond with their age." Hiding behind this ambiguous wording was the fact that they were required to perform soldiers' duties while "legally considered" to be mere helpers, assistants, or support personnel. He feels strongly that this was another example of how the Nazis treated "legalities" as a basis for the authority to draft minors into combat duty, seeing it only as a means to "final victory."

The futility of children serving at the front had no end, for within 10 days of the war's conclusion, the national Hitler Youth leader declared, "From the Hitler Youth has emerged a movement of young tank busters....There is only victory or annihilation. Know no bounds in your love to your people; equally, know no bounds in your hatred of the enemy. It is your duty....your greatest honor, however, is your unshakable faithfulness to Adolf Hitler."[11]

Jungvolk members such as H. Pfrengle had little choice. One unit near Berlin in the last days of the war reported, "...Our leader...and the police fetched us from our homes....My *Jungzugfuehrer* who refused was strung up on the nearest tree by a few SS men and an SA man. But then he was already fifteen years old...."[12]

Chapter 1

Looking for My Father:
My First Years

I was born on August 2, 1929, in Stuttgart, Germany, the capital of the then state of Wuerttemberg. That state takes a special place in German history in that the former kingdom of Wuerttemberg was the first one to adopt, as a result of the 1848 liberal revolution, a semi-democratic constitution with a bicameral parliament. I am still proud that my parents picked for my birthplace this picturesquely situated and architecturally interesting city, where the old Romans had built spas and enjoyed the good life already two thousand years ago.

My mother, Luise Schneider nee Karle, came from a religious Protestant family in the rural area east of Karlsruhe, where her father ran a small trading business. Her upbringing in a tightly knit communal environment that stressed, above all, God-fearing modesty, law-abiding civility, and adherence to traditional moral, religious, and family values shaped her character and personality which I, and later my half-brother Roland Pfrengle, would often perceive as being overly rigid and authoritarian during our formative years. It took me many years of maturing to really understand and appreciate what my mother had done for me, and us.

My father, Wilhelm Schneider, a business administrator by profession, came from a more mundane and wealthy family of industrial entrepreneurs who had been among the cofounders of the MAN Machine Factory Augsburg-Nuernberg. As his mother proudly told me later, they owned one of the first automobiles in the late 1800s in Augsburg. But young Wilhelm aspired not after a career in engineering and production. Rather, the lure of the wide world made him become an administrator of a German farm in New Guinea.

1

Following his call to arms in World War I, he returned to Germany and lost his left leg in combat (ironically, 73 years later I lost my left leg due to a skiing accident). In the wake of the lost war, the German economy was in ruins, war reparations were sapping the last lifeblood from what was left of the German industrial and financial base, unemployment was near 30 percent, and hyperinflation was rampant. The Schneiders, like many wealthy entrepreneurial families, had lost their family fortune.

My earliest childhood memories go back to age two or three: once I climbed on a window sill of our fifth floor apartment, opened the window wing, and took in the fascinating sight of traffic moving on the street below. The next thing I remember is that my mother came from behind, grabbed me and put an abrupt end to my scenic adventure. On another occasion, the lure of the big, wide world made me set out on a long walk to find out what was behind the familiar surroundings of our block and playground. Sitting by railroad tracks, I watched trains go to and from. After night had fallen, I became scared, wandered about, crying for my mother until a police patrol picked me up and turned me over to her in the middle of the night. She had been equally scared, but saw fit to give me a memorable spanking even before we returned home, putting a painful end to such excursions for the time being.

In many respects, the characters and personalities of my mother and father were too different to make for a lasting marriage, and my mother divorced him when I was three. I enjoyed some of his visits after the divorce, when he came to play with me. But my mother objected to his visits. She did everything in her power to make me forget about him, and I had to get used to a life without a father.

My mother and I moved to the Stuttgart suburb of Bad Cannstatt where she took a job as a shop worker, and later as an office assistant, trying hard to make a living. Kindergarten opened up a new world for me, but sometimes my mother was too exhausted to deal with me after she had come home after a hard day's work, and eventually, some loving and understanding relatives would take me to their farm for longer periods of time. Those stays at the farm were the happiest times of my early childhood.

Not least to my prodding, or so I thought ("Mama, we are going to marry this uncle, right?"), my mother in 1935 married Dr. Otto

H. Pfrengle at age eight at
home in Budenheim, 1937

The Pfrengle family, 1938.
Mother, Luise; adoptive father,
Otto; Hermann

Pfrengle, a chemist, who came from a patriotic-minded middle-class family whose home was near Lake Constance. We moved to Budenheim, a small (wartime population about 3,500) semi-rural town near Mainz where my new father had found a job as a chemist at the Oetker Chemical Company. I quickly came to love him. One of the first things he did, as a matter of pride and newly acquired parental authority, was to cancel my natural father's child support payments for me. He helped me to build model airplanes and other things exciting a boy's imagination and creativity. Saturday afternoons, after my father had returned from work, were usually set aside for these joint father-son activities which I looked forward to all week long.[1] There were weekend family hikes through the Taunus mountains, ending with a rest stop at one of the many *Strausswirtschaften*, simple rural inns where food and drink was cheap, and where my father enjoyed his weekly glass of Rheingau wine. We picked mushrooms in the forests (the frugal family budget made my mother equate the nutritional value of a cup of mushrooms with a veal cutlet). Summer steamboat trips on the Rhine, ice skating in the winter—all in all it was a happy and carefree time for me. We grew together into one joyful family. As our life-style gradually improved materially, my parents moved to a better apartment with its own garden which my mother enjoyed tending to, and where I raised a few rabbits, not for pets, but extra meat.

I attended elementary school in Budenheim from 1936 to 1939. My parents saw to it that I was always close to the top of my class. School per se was not a great challenge for me. Rather, the challenge came when I expressed the desire to have certain things, e.g., an erector set, a toy train, or an Indian chief's costume for carnival: I first had to "earn" these things by bringing home good grades. This educational principle instilled in me an early sense of self-discipline to achieve a goal, and of how the world worked. However, it was not only my mother's sometimes overbearing manners, but also a feeling of thankful cooperation to do my share that made me light the coal fire in the kitchen stove first thing in the morning, or help with cooking chores. On a more practical level, my display of cooperation also helped to reduce chances of getting punished for swiping home-made cookies at Christmas time.

True to his parents' "traditional" values my father was a patriot. He proudly told me that he had written the German essay for

his high school graduation in 1919—one year after Germany's de
feat in World War I—on the topic of the British slogan, "Right or
Wrong—My Country!" Like most Germans at the time, he saw in
Hitler the leader who had been able to revive Germany behind the
uniting patriotic idea of the *Vaterland* (Fatherland), rebuild its
economy, and provide work for the masses. Out of this conviction
my father had joined the Nazi Brownshirts in the early 1930s. In his
view, it was only right that Hitler later reunited the Rhineland and
the Saarland with the rest of the Fatherland.

In 1938, my father and I took a train trip to Frankfurt where
Hitler was to attend a big Nazi festivity. My father did not wear his
Brownshirt uniform (in fact, I saw him wear it only once). After the
crowds had yelled for a long time "We want to see our *Fuehrer*," a
third- or fourth-story window in a big building opened, and the
Fuehrer appeared for perhaps 10 or 20 seconds, saluting the crowds
with the angular stiffness of a half-raised right arm. I saw him from
a distance of perhaps one hundred meters (the only time I saw him
in person). After the frenzy had subsided, I felt a little disappointed.
Shortly after, I noticed a change in my father's behavior. He became
pensive, and wouldn't play with me as much as he used to, though
he still played a game of chess with me, talked about history or books
I was reading, now and then. My mother explained to me that he
had been promoted at his job, and the added responsibility left him
less time for play. Years later I learned that he had decided then to
quit the Nazi Brownshirt movement. Though he would never elaborate on his motive, I am pretty certain it was disillusionment with
the course the Nazi party was steering then. The onset of Hitler's
megalomania, the Anschluss of Austria and "returning the
Sudetenland to the Fatherland" may also have had something to do
with his decision. Around that time he was drafted as a member of
the *Flak* reserve to training exercises, where he broke an arm. "The
Fatherland's first new casualty," he would joke afterwards.

Eventually life left me with less time to play, too, after I had
passed in April 1939, together with two other elementary school
classmates, the entrance examination to the *Realgymnasium* in
Mainz.[2] I became a train commuter student, and usually didn't get
home from school until mid-afternoon. No more warm lunches in
mother's cozy kitchen; sandwiches my mother stuffed into my satchel

had to do. The rest of the day was filled with homework and chores around the house, followed, perhaps, by some free time. This had become the iron order of things as established by the family's code of discipline.

My exposure to a new peer group in Mainz also acquainted me with Nazi-supported youth activities. Some of my new classmates proudly wore the *Jungvolk* brown shirt, and told exciting stories about summer camps, sports events, and marching behind a Hitler Youth band.[3] I talked my parents into putting in a word for me so I could join up with the *Jungvolk* in Budenheim, although I wasn't 10 yet. The boys who joined with me were those born in the first half of 1929, about all those boys of that age group I knew. My friends came mostly from the immediate neighborhood and all walks of life.

I got my first brown shirt only after my grades had improved and after I had reached the compulsory membership age of 10. Once I had become a *Jungvolk* member, and after my father adopted me the same year, thus removing the stigma of still bearing a last name which was synonymous with the failure of my mother's first marriage, I felt fully accepted by my peers and society. This boosted my self-assurance tremendously.

Chapter 2

Gaining Self-Assurance:
Service in the *Jungvolk*

Most parents thought joining the *Jungvolk* was a good idea to instill some "law-and-order" attitudes, and discipline, in their children. Sports events and other forms of competition were welcomed as adding to physical education and development, and so were certain *Jungvolk* activities such as helping farmers bring in the fall harvests, free of charge to them, collecting for the needy, or other kinds of community service. Some parents were more reserved and didn't allow their boys to attend all the *Jungvolk* meetings and would send a written excuse. By fear of isolation from the rest of their *Kumpels* (buddies), or being deemed a "pariah," some boys insisted on attending against their parents' wishes, as at least that is what a few friends hinted.

I joined the *Jungvolk* in April 1939 in a joyous initiation rite. Apart of the rite, we new members had to promise our local *Jungvolk Faehnleinfuehrer* (top leader) who was about 16 or 17 years old, to be tough, faithful, good comrades, and that our highest value would be honor. I was rather serious about being a member of the *Jungvolk*. It gave a young boy something worthwhile and imaginative to do, I was with my friends, and it was interesting and fun.

There was not much of indoctrination in national socialism, usually from some visitor, and "politics" per se was a "dirty word." Of course, we were all susceptible to propaganda at the time, and had little recourse but to accept much of what we were told by authorities as being true. We were impressionable, and we were being bent to be nationalistic. Not until 1943–44, as we started to become aware of some of the contradictions in Nazi claims and its system,

Father, Dr. Otto Pfrengle, *Luftwaffe Flak* reservist, ca. 1938

in light of the war's events turning against Germany, did I and some of my comrades begin to see things more critically. Too, we were maturing and hopefully more capable of seeing for ourselves.

On September 1, 1939, the small town of Budenheim was strangely quiet. War had broken out. I heard the news on the radio that morning, and that school had been canceled for the day. As I went shopping, I saw serious-faced groups of people talking in low voices. The *Fuehrer* had announced that the Germans were tired of being shot at, and from now on would shoot back at the Poles. The mood in town was depressed, even fearful. Draft orders for men in Budenheim arrived more frequently. My father was mobilized and reported to a *Flak* unit in Mainz, where he served as a communications specialist. Upon his employer's request, he was discharged as a corporal in mid-1940 and resumed his work as a chemist. Civil defense and black-out regulations went into effect. Buckets with sand and water had to be kept in attics to fight fires in the event the "enemy" would drop incendiary bombs.

The "enemy"—this was still an elusive, and confusing concept to me. In official announcements Nazi propaganda referred to the "enemy" in ideological terms, such as the "Imperialists," "Plutocrats," "Bolsheviks," the "Forces of Darkness." So which of the four were we fighting in Poland? Probably the Bolsheviks, I concluded, because Poland was geographically so close to the Soviet Union. But why did all of these enemies suddenly gang up on Germany?

By the end of the *Blitzkrieg* in Poland a few weeks later, people felt some relief. The initial shock of war was giving way to purposive optimism. Many thought it would all be over soon. "Well, perhaps France will best stay out of it," people said, and some added spitefully, "unless the 'Forces of Darkness' ruling that country will surrender. Anyway, the record for World War I will be set straight." But that would be it; the war would be over then.

Now the *Fuehrer* had brought back to the Fatherland all the German territory of which it had been robbed by the unjust Treaty of Versailles: the Rhineland, Sudetenland, Saarland, and Warthegau (comprising the regions of Danzig, Posen, Breslau, and Upper Silesia, all occupied by Poland after World War I). We boys thought that the *Fuehrer*, in righting these wrongs, had reestablished justice for the German people and deserved admiration for that.

England wouldn't pose a serious threat to Germany because it was an island, and our U-boats would take care of "John Bull's" strong navy. And, after all, couldn't we feel safe from enemy air raids because *Reichsmarschall* Hermann Goering, the commander in chief of the *Luftwaffe*, himself had vowed to change his name to "Meier" if even one enemy aircraft would enter German airspace?[1]

Goering's vow seemed to hold for some months, and, indeed, the first aircraft mistakenly downed by *Flak* in the Mainz area was not an enemy one, but a German *Messerschmitt*. According to the *Wehrmachtsberichte,* German forces were in firm control on all fronts.[2] German U-boats were sinking "enemy" ships in the Atlantic. I wondered to myself how much more could it take to convince the enemy to make peace now, rather than suffer defeat like Poland.

I vaguely recall a news item around November 10, 1939, about a failed attempt on Hitler's life. Surrounded by many of his early party followers, he was giving a speech commemorating his first and ill-fated grasp at local power in Munich in 1923. The place was the *Hofbraeuhaus,* both a popular Bavarian beer hall and an old Nazi hangout (by the way, Hitler was said to have been anti-alcohol and a vegetarian whose favorite dish was eggs sunny-side-up, spinach, and potatoes). But for some unknown reason, he cut his speech short and left earlier than scheduled, thus avoiding a planted bomb's powerful explosion that killed several of his friends and injured many others. I was initially disturbed at hearing about this cowardly attempt on the *Fuehrer*, but gave it no more thought because afterwards he ascribed his "salvation" to "divine providence." As God still took the highest level in my infantile imagination of a universal power hierarchy, I left it at that. If God was on the *Fuehrer*'s side— and apparently He was—nothing could go wrong with Germany.

The reality of war was increasingly reflected in my *Jungvolk* activities which included training in camouflaging, taking cover in terrain, and administering first aid. As for the rest of our training, we learned to pitch tents, build open fires, read maps, the stars, and the compass. We participated in sports, swimming and air gun target shooting competitions, summer camps, and cross-country hikes— pretty much typical activities that any Boy Scouts would do. (Boy Scouts in Germany had been organized into various groups and brands: political, Catholic, Protestant, or "free thinking"—not as homogeneously organized and structured as in the United States.)

Training was led by older *Jungvolk* leaders or occasionally by a member of the *Wehrmacht* in a one-to-two-hour session. Our group of about one hundred boys also had to learn to recite the *Fuehrer's* biography in brief, a litany which was part of a test. We also sang a lot of *Volkslieder* (folk songs), a few songs about the Nazis' rise to power, and military marching songs when we were trying to impress people, such as during our marches through town at the end of our usual Saturday afternoon meetings. Most of us thoroughly enjoyed these activities. When once in a while a Nazi *Goldfasan*[3] from Mainz came to give our group an indoctrination speech about honor, duty to the Fatherland, Nazi ideals, and other propaganda slogans, we took this in good stride, silently looking forward to our next outing or sports event. Later I have often thought about the fatal consequences of the statement of Hitler in his biography: "In 1919, I decided to become a politician."

Once war broke out, the Hitler Youth acted to streamline the *Jungvolk* and Hitler Youth organizationally by eliminating some of the strict divisions, but the separation between them continued at least in my region of Mainz, and Budenheim especially, throughout the war, though perhaps not as strictly as before. For one thing, the 15–18 year olds could choose membership among the Hitler Youth's various technical branches for aviation, naval, and automotive. We *Jungvolk* boys wished we could have had similar choices to accommodate our interests and preferences, but ours was to do the menial work, including collecting for the war effort scrap metal, bottles, and paper, helping in money drives for the poor, and assisting farmers. During the war's first year we even had to be home at dark most of the time whereas the older Hitler Youth did not.

Informed by the official news that Hitler had decided to support Germany's close ally Mussolini (*Il Duce*, Italy's *"Fuehrer"*) militarily in the Balkans, where an Italian campaign against Albania and Greece had stalemated in late 1940, some people in Budenheim, my parents included, began to wonder if Germany wasn't spreading its forces too thin. Such opinions could be voiced confidentially only, of course, because any open criticism of the *Fuehrer's* decision could have resulted in severe punishment. True, the Budenheim community as I knew it certainly was no Nazi hotbed of spies and informers, but one had to be careful nevertheless.

The more I tuned my ears to catch a lead into the grown-ups' hidden world of thought, and the more inquisitive I became, also the more reclusive their attitudes and responses became. Many of my *Jungvolk* comrades felt the same way. At our occasional *Kameradschaftszusammenkuenfte* (companionable meetings of comrades), unsupervised by higher ranks, we could speak more freely among ourselves. The meetings became not only a kind of relief valve for what bothered us, but also a sort of informal information exchange. While being a middle-rank *Jungvolk* leader at the time, in those meetings I chose to make myself rankless, giving way to a democratic instinct. It was our way of "brainstorming." I never had the feel I lost their respect. Contrarily, I am sure I thus gained more of it when playing my usual role as their leader. It was mutual. I learned early on that respect cannot be regulated or ordered; it must be earned continuously.

As to the issue about helping the Italians, some people felt that, by the old Germanic rule to stick to a friend when he is in need, Germany should come to their aid. If nothing else it would prove to them that their historian Tacitus was right when he wrote two thousand years ago that with the Germans a firm handshake was more meaningful than sworn oaths with the tricky Romans. Other Germans sneered that the Italians were better lovers than fighters, and our country should not shoulder the extra burden of helping them getting out of trouble, which was their own making anyway.

If memory serves me right, the local opinions about the Italians weren't much different in early 1941 after Germany had restored Axis control in the Balkans. Italy then needed our help again, this time in its ill-considered North African campaign which *Il Duce* had plunged into in 1939. German help led to the creation of the *Afrikakorps* under the command of Field Marshal Erwin Rommel, the "Desert Fox," and the diversion of hundreds of thousands of *Wehrmacht* forces and many aircraft, much heavy material, equipment, and transportation resources to that front. These resources would not be available to Hitler, for his campaign against the Soviet Union launched a few months later. Some historians argue that without the German engagement in North Africa, Hitler could have started his Soviet campaign as early as the spring of 1941, as was the original plan. The outcome might have been decided in his favor by the time the extremely cold winter had exhausted his troops just short of Moscow.

Back in Budenheim, by 1943, popular wisdom had reached a similar conclusion. A group of people, who had initially scoffed at the Italians, grew larger and openly ridiculed them and their poor military performance in North Africa: "Why the devil did we help a country whose engineers design vehicles with reverse gears only?"

At school, we went through air-raid and fire drills, and up to 1943, school was not significantly disrupted by enemy air activities. But some of our younger teachers were drafted, to be replaced by older rigid substitutes who didn't hesitate to get their academic point across with the help of a slap on the face. Mathematics, English, Latin, arts, and sports were my favorite subjects then. At home, my father had taught me chess, and when I began beating him around age 12, he wouldn't play me anymore.

In the spring of 1940, we heard in the official news that Britain had started to disrupt German raw materials shipments in Norwegian territorial waters. Special newscasts in April reported the British also were laying mines there and landing troops in Norway, and that sea battles between our navies were underway. But the reports emphasized, as I recall, German army and paratrooper units who had landed in Norway to drive out the British. The battles of Narvik, where about four thousand Germans, without a logistics supply line, held out against a vastly superior enemy, became the symbol of German victory in the Norwegian campaign. At home, we looked at this victory as yet another lesson the *Fuehrer* taught tricky "John Bull" (a nickname for Britain). How many more bloody noses would it take until the Bull settled peacefully in his own pen? (The irony of this question didn't become apparent to me until years later.) For now, Hitler had reined in Britain's imperialistic expansionism, and this event received special treatment in my history course at school.

The cultural center at Budenheim was the movie theater with an adjoining pub and restaurant. Until about 1942, it showed a new movie every other week or so, and about once a month my parents and I went to see one. It was a very special event I looked forward to with great excitement. The show opened with a 15–20-minute newsreel with scenes usually from the *Wehrmacht*'s latest victories; demonstrations of new military equipment; some outstanding civilian accomplishments such as in sports, mountaineering, or charitable work; and snapshots of the *Fuehrer* and high-ranking dignitaries at work, attending social functions, visiting hospitals, and receiving delegations from abroad, or from various party organizations. To partake at least for a few minutes in some of the great events about the Reich, its leadership and heroes, was a breathtaking and impressionable experience for me. The main film, about 90 minutes long on average, usually showed the story of a great German scientist, inventor, or other famous historical figure.

With the onset of the war, stories about German military heroes, or the liberation of German population oppressed by foreign occupation under the "Dictate of Versailles," were shown more frequently. I dimly remember the heartrending portrayal of ethnic Germans who were persecuted and expropriated in the formerly German part of Poland. In the year before the *Wehrmacht* moved into Poland, thousands had fled from the Polish Corridor into Germany and East Prussia. For almost 20 years, Germany had requested a free access road to its enclaves of East Prussia and Danzig, landlocked since 1919. But Poland stubbornly and arrogantly rejected this seemingly modest and reasonable request. So I thought the *Fuehrer* was right in putting an end to his ongoing humiliation of Germans and Germany.

Another movie geared to events in the campaigns was a story about a German sergeant (played by well-known actor Rene Deltgen) who single-handedly silenced a British machine gun nest in Norway after the British had landed there first in the spring of 1940 in violation of Norwegian neutrality, and in an effort to cut off Scandinavian raw materials shipments to Germany. The sergeant died a war hero, his brave act helping to drive the numerically superior British forces out of Norway. But perhaps due to my parents' choice of movies, I don't recall watching such hero stories often.

The year 1940 also brought the German *Blitzkrieg* defeat of France. This would be it, then, people thought. Let the British sit on their island until they were ready to make peace. Hadn't the *Fuehrer*, by abruptly halting the final German blow on hundreds of thousands of British troops encircled in the Dunkirk area, given them a chance to flee across the English Channel in a hasty one-week evacuation using all sorts of boats dispatched from the island? We were sure that the whole world could now see how generous Hitler really was, and that he wasn't bent on destroying a helpless enemy, not even forcing him to surrender. He demonstrated to the arrogant Englishmen what a real gentleman was like, a term whose property they claimed as a national characteristic of their very own!

As I recollect these early war impressions, there was indeed a difference in how Nazi propaganda and the media made us perceive the enemies. England used to come off better than France or Russia. Lending support to this impression is also the dramatic attempt of Rudolf Hess, Hitler's first deputy, to make peace with Britain on his own by flying all by himself to England in May 1941, parachuting in northern England, and requesting his British captors notify some of his English friends with whom he had been in secret contact during the war. But the British were not interested in negotiating with Hess.

Years after the war I read about a kind of love-hate relationship that Hitler had entertained toward Britain, and he may have been predisposed to it by a real love relationship with an Englishwoman, Lady Unity Mitford, in the 1930s. She was a niece of Winston Churchill. Infatuated with Hitler, his early Nazi ideals, and initial peace policy, she maintained her romantic passion and pleaded with him for peace until the day he invaded Poland. On that day, September 1, 1939, she committed suicide in Munich's English Garden, a romantic and beautiful public park frequented by lovers. This love relationship and its tragic ending could have provided ample material for a Wagneresque opera, the kind of music Hitler loved above all. If there really was this love-hate relationship, it is safe to assume that it had lost its element of love by the time the Royal Air Force started bombing the German population. Then England's preferential treatment by Nazi propaganda and the media ceased, and she became an enemy portrayed as mean, cruel, and bad as the rest of them.

What I recall about the above Hess escapade is merely a brief note in the official German news saying that Hess had acted on his own and in a state of "mental derangement." One of my father's colleagues, who was not known for being a Nazi supporter, commented dryly and somewhat ambiguously: "Yep, even leaders in the highest places can get sick."

The German victories had made it easier for people to adapt psychologically, and nutritionally, to wartime life. We figured some sacrifices at home were in order to assure an early and successful end to the war. Ration cards for food, clothing, tobacco, alcohol, and coal—the general household fuel—had come to be accepted as a normal fact of life.[4] Once coffee became rationed also, many a woman, my mother included, discovered a taste for "real" coffee (which came mostly from sources in Holland)—as distinct from *Ersatzkaffee* (substitute coffee)—and insisted that they had to have it to keep their *Kaffeeklatsche* (coffee gossip sessions) going. But eventually, even such private get-togethers took on a more serious orientation, such as repairing old clothes, baking cakes for the wounded in hospitals, supporting wives whose husbands had been killed in action, and trading ration card sections, a prohibited activity which, nevertheless, the people felt was necessary so that an underground economy could operate on the principle of supply and demand.

Hermann Pfrengle with his mother, Luise, 1939

I find it very difficult today to gauge my parents' feelings and thoughts at the time. They had become more serious, in a way more aloof from things. My father lost his temper more easily if my grades at school did not live up to his expectations. My parents must have yearned for the simple happiness of the all-too-few prewar years in their rather harmonious marriage. They never seemed to be really jubilant at the announcement of yet another German war victory. But likewise, they never seemed to express strong anti-Nazi sentiment, or views, in my presence (today, of course, I understand why they would not, or could not, even if they had wanted to. Such expression would have been a criminal act). Sure, occasionally they would voice doubts or uncertainties when I prodded them for answers to inconvenient questions. But they also evaded many direct answers and referred me to the news about events to come. Often, I believe, they didn't know the answers either. Today I would say that they came under the category of citizens known as the "silent majority."

Germany's early military successes in the Balkans, North Africa, and the Soviet Union boosted people's hopes that final victory was near. Some citizens weren't so sure, however, and those who had lost a family member in combat were silent altogether in their sadness and grief.[5] There were more questions about what were the goals, and when? From a home-front perspective, there was no denying that the gradually increasing frequency and severity of Allied air raids on Western and Northern Germany brought the war to the people's doorsteps. Thus the feeling of security generated by imagining the great distances between the foreign lands where the German armies won battle after battle, and the safety of one's life at home, gave way to the realization of direct confrontation and death. Our neighbor's basement was structurally reinforced to serve as a bomb shelter for our block, and I vividly remember the many times my family and neighbors congregated there during air raids any time of the day or night, equipped with gas masks and first-aid kits.

I guessed that our neighbor's basement was reinforced as an air raid shelter not only because of its relatively large size, but also because the neighbor, Dr. Kuhn, was a *Luftwaffe* officer in Berlin. A chemist and my father's former colleague, he served in the *Reichsluftfahrtministerium*, the Reich Aviation Ministry, headed by Hermann Goering. Dr. Kuhn managed to come home for the Christmas holidays, and he always invited my family over for New Year's celebrations. He impressed me with his bluish *Luftwaffe* uniform, decorated with a couple of medals, and I eagerly listened to his stories relating to service in Berlin. At first they sounded impressive, sometimes humorous. But in the last three years of the war, I noticed growing dissatisfaction in his words about how things were going in Berlin and elsewhere. I tuned my ears hoping to hear something heroic or exciting that would boost my *Jungvolk* idealism, which lately had become a little shaky. But any such boosts failed to materialize, and I grew tired of hearing such unpleasant grown-up talk that often made my father pensive, and me very eager to indulge in the sweets Dr. Kuhn had brought. A place that still had such goodies couldn't be all that bad, his daughters and I thought.

When the German campaign fizzled in the snow and cold of the Russian winter in 1941–42, a nationwide household collection of all kinds of supply items was called in support of our troops in Russia. Thus went my beloved bicycle and binoculars and my father's skis and boots, along with blankets and sweaters. What really saddened me, though, was that the *Fuehrer* didn't take better care of our troops out there. That I could not understand.

A short time later I had the opportunity of observing the lavish life-style in some higher-up Nazi circles when I attended youth leadership training and selection courses near Mainz and Frankfurt.[6] What I came to see in their activities was in stark contrast to the reality of war as the ordinary people experienced it. They commanded a plentiful supply of food, alcohol, and gasoline for their official cars in which they sometimes took their loves, beautiful Hitler Youth girls, on rides. I felt disenchantment for a while until my father hinted at the possibility that Nazism and the "Fatherland" might not always be one and the same thing—it all depended upon whose standards were being used at the time.

Nationwide collections of money for charity at home had

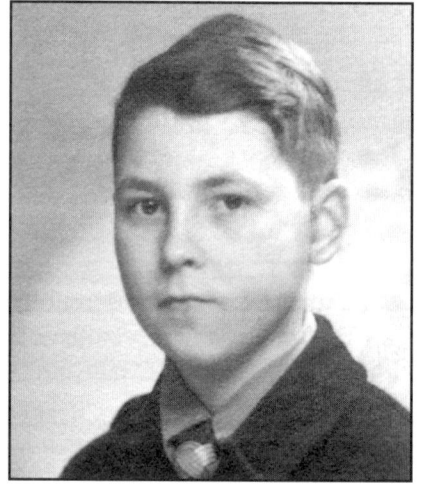

H. Pfrengle in 1940

become the rule for several winters now. The biggest drive, the *Winterhilfswerk* (Winter Relief Effort), meant for the neediest of the needy and bombed-out families, used lists of names of household heads who then were required to enter the amount of money they were willing to give. Members of local youth organizations carried these lists and sealed collection cans from household to household and block to block. The lists were open for everyone to see, a clever psychological catch that played on people's pride at not being outdone or shamed by poorer neighbors. Everybody could readily see how much everybody else had donated or pledged. Some people took a long time studying the names and amounts before deciding which of their neighbors they wanted, or could afford, to live up to. But playing on neighbors' competitiveness didn't always work. Still, we boys felt a certain pride of accomplishment as we delivered the often well-filled money cans to the town hall after long hours. The *Winterhilfswerk* motto literally translated was, "Nobody shall starve or freeze!" As living conditions worsened in general, and charitable organizations brought less and less relief, popular humor found another sarcastic vein by changing the motto to, "Nobody shall starve without freezing!"

In 1943, I spent my six-week summer vacation at a *Rittergut*, a huge manor/farm combination in Thuringia where a cousin of mine worked as an administrative assistant. I worked as a farm hand among a bunch of young people. Some of the young men and older boys eyed me with caution and a certain reservation, perhaps because my cousin had told them I was a *Jungvolk* leader. Personally, I liked most of them and tried hard to fit in. After a couple of weeks they opened up to me, and I was pretty shocked to hear that some of them were outright anti-Nazi, especially the older ones whose call to arms had been deferred because they were close to graduating from high school or college, perhaps of a religious nature, or so they told me. One of them contemptuously spoke of the "Hitler-*Schweine*." This was almost too much for me to tolerate, but with the help of my cousin and a parson's daughter, my first love, I came to realize that I was dealing with a new group of people, very different from what I had been used to so far, and I couldn't help but respect them for their courage to voice contradictions to my belief system which had become a little shaky as of late. I countered by saying that they could talk like this in the protected seclusion of the *Rittergut*, but not in the outside world. "Eventually we will," they said.[7]

I pondered over such displays of civil disobedience and disdain toward the *Fuehrer* and the Reich. How could otherwise seemingly nice and friendly people say such forbidden and shocking things!? I struggled to find an answer to this tormenting contradiction. Then pieces of a dimly remembered episode from my earlier childhood began to take on a clearer shape and slowly fall into place. Hadn't my own godfather aroused some family members' wrath about a year before the war started when he openly and disgustedly scorned Nazi behavior in Stuttgart? Uncle Hermann, my mother's brother-in-law, was wiry, quick-witted, and outspoken. His strict, often disciplining manners inspired me with awe whenever I spent a week or two with the childless couple before the war. He had dropped out of a Jesuit seminary, took up this-worldly pursuits and now owned a barber shop in Stuttgart.

One day in 1938 the Nazis wanted him to put a sticker reading *"Deutsches Geschaeft"* (German business) and display a swastika on his shop's window. This was, of course, part of the ongoing Nazi discrimination against Jewish-owned businesses. But Uncle Hermann refused to do so, arguing that he was German, his folks were German, his business was German, and therefore he didn't need such a sign. He got into some trouble when he continued to steadfastly refuse to obey that Nazi decree. Shortly thereafter he either sold his business, or the Nazis closed it. He and Aunt Emma moved away and he ended up in the German army. I remember how this event had infuriated him, how some family folks tended to ascribe his emotional and rebellious behavior to his stubbornness and hotheadedness, and how taciturn and reserved he became when later I tried to prod him for more details about this episode. Some in our family remarked casually that every family had its black sheep. But Uncle Hermann stood up for his conviction and demonstrated more than just passive "inner resistance" to ward off a regime he couldn't identify with. Today I admire my godfather for his courage and strength of conviction to act as he did. But then, in a 13-year-old boy's mind, doubts began to stir.

I returned home from the *Rittergut* with some nagging thoughts in my mind about whether the Nazis' "just cause" was always "just." My *Jungvolk* rank in 1944 was *Hauptjungzugfuehrer*, the number two in charge of about 150 boys. As a leader, I could influence and shape the form and content of our *Jungvolk* meetings to an extent, and began to de-emphasize Nazi propaganda aspects. Of course, that did not mean I openly opposed the Nazi regime: that might have been suicidal, or at least would have caused my parents much trouble. As the war wound on, it was easier to emphasize the more practical aspects of our membership, such as firefighting, rescue exercises, first aid, helping farmers with the harvest, or to take cover from air attacks.

When a classmate of mine made fun of a Jewish woman in Mainz who wore a yellow Star of David on her coat, I struck him in the face. My parents felt uneasy when I kept bringing up the subject of "Right or Wrong—My Country." My father felt the emphasis should be on saving the country. But how?

In our small town of Budenheim, the "top Nazi" was our *Buergermeister*, a man of outstanding humane qualities. In other words, there were Nazis, and there were "Nazis." (My rough estimate is that in Budenheim in 1939–40, there were about 20–30 Nazi members, mostly middle-aged men.)

My mother sought closer ties to the local Protestant church at the time, whereas my father was largely areligious (noncommittal or professedly neutral) by his parents' tradition. To him, religious belief began where science left off, and eventually everything would become explainable by scientific means. My mother urged him to attend Sunday church together with her, and, to make her happy, he would occasionally come along. He also acquiesced in the rituals accompanying my Protestant church confirmation.

In Budenheim, the Catholic Church and the *Jungvolk* mutually tolerated each other by some degree. I recall that in 1944, I scheduled our regular Saturday afternoon *Jungvolk* meetings so that Catholics (the population was about 85-percent Catholic) could go to confession, and as war-related duties extended our meeting times I gave them permission to quit early for that purpose. I also vividly remember the day in 1944 when Catholic dissent had reached Budenheim. Walking past the church after a meeting, three of my *Jungenschaftsfuehrer* (in charge of 10–12 boys each) spontaneously handed over their rank insignia to me. Shocked and stunned, I asked them why. They replied something about being altar boys, and ran

H. Pfrengle's mother in their home, Budenheim, 1939

away and disappeared behind the protective walls of the 18th-century church building. I left it at that, with a feeling of indignation and contempt, but deep inside it hurt because I had trusted them completely in the belief that they shared the good cause of the organization with me. All three were high school/junior college students like me, and I had come to appreciate their contributions towards raising training and education standards of their *Jungenschaft* groups.

I am sure that this demonstrative dissent was orchestrated by and coordinated with the local priest. In retrospect, it dawned on me why he would change to the other side of the street whenever we were walking toward each other. Obviously he wished to avoid me. I felt that there was a "dark force" behind the church's ancient thick walls, something more powerful than I could handle. What stuck with me was that I, as a Protestant, became impressed with the strength of the Catholic belief system.

By 1943, the Allied air forces ruled the German skies. On clear days we used to count the *Liberators* and *Flying Fortresses* by the hundreds as their groups and wings were heading in undisturbed, paradelike formation, toward yet another carpet bombing target. Up to the summer of 1943, their flight paths were quite often accentuated

H. Pfrengle's Budenheim *Jungvolk* group on a march, early summer 1944. He carries the flag. *To his right,* Eduard Hellmeister; *to his left,* Arno Karger

by the white puffs of 88mm anti-aircraft shells exploding harmlessly at their maximum effective range, about 500 to 1,000 meters below their unreachable targets. The newly fielded longer-range 127mm anti-aircraft guns were ineffective, too, because they were few in numbers, and the bombers would just fly a few notches higher. What good were the 20mm and 37mm *Flak* batteries that had taken positions around Budenheim, on and off, since 1939? They just sat there, waiting for low-flying aircraft which never came.[8]

One night one of them came, though. I remember a night air raid on the Mainz area, and the sight of a burning four-engine American bomber, its engines roaring, circling almost overhead at an altitude of less than 1,000 meters, illuminated by several *Flak* searchlight beams. Watching from our backyard, I was fascinated by the fireworks as the light *Flak* cannons spewed tracers at their target. My mother's warning cry to come inside was drowned out by the explosions of bombs being dumped in an emergency. I don't know what kept me watching so breathlessly, all by myself. Perhaps it was the desire to witness some sort of German "victory" over the enemy, or a universal youthful desire to be part of the action. The sight of about eight men jumping from the aircraft in split-second intervals, their parachutes unfolding about halfway to the ground, was the last thing I remember about this direct-action drama, and before the plane crashed in a dull explosion behind some trees.

After this exciting action ended, I felt like I had personally accomplished a special act. I had proved that I would not run from danger and hide in a basement. My newly gained pride was then somewhat shaken when my father remarked that my insistence on watching the fireworks spectacle was not a demonstration of heroism, but stupidity.

Next morning we *Jungvolk* received orders to search for crew members of that bomber or other aircraft shot down. A local police deputy who wore a pistol accompanied us. Finally we could put our *Jungvolk* scouting practice to the real test, we boys thought. But all we found in the woods west of Budenheim were some small empty cardboard boxes and food cans with English inscriptions on them. We looked with some kind of awe at this sign of an enemy presence presumed so close, and yet, because they were invisible, so far. Apparently they had been surprised and hastily fled from this site, leaving their trash behind unburied. I am sure they must have been captured some place, somehow, though I never heard any more about them.

A day or two later I went to see that plane's nearby crash site. It was guarded by soldiers who would not allow anyone to get close. Perhaps there still were live bombs amidst the wreckage. My initial excitement about those spectacular fireworks gave way to the sobering realization that the *Flak* had caught one, but hundreds had escaped unharmed.

I built a wooden scale model of the Boeing *Flying Fortress*, based on aircraft identification charts which became a new topic for our *Jungvolk* meetings. Soon we knew the various enemy and friendly aircraft types by heart. But what good would that be if we couldn't defend ourselves against Allied aircraft? Mainz had been hit hard twice already, with thousands of civilians killed and about 25 percent of the city in ruins. My school was damaged, but classes continued. With little or no heat the next winter, bundled up in layers of sweaters and overcoats (I wore my mother's old one), we learned about the Spartans' last stand at the Thermopylae but didn't dare openly draw comparisons to the German Fatherland's visible demise. The teachers mostly conformed with Nazi instructions emphasizing heroic deeds and self-sacrifice in the interest of saving the Fatherland.[9] And true to the principle that one ought to practice what one teaches, my Latin teacher, who had lost a leg in World War I, joined the Nazi party 10 months before the end of the war.

During the early war most of my school teachers were fairly young or middle-aged. They, not their older colleagues, inspired students' interests in particular subjects, in my case mathematics, arts, and sports. We could identify with them as role models. Unfortunately most of them were drafted into war service, and an older guard of teachers took over, a few recalled from retirement. Corporal punishment was the exception rather than the rule, but many an old *Pauker* (crammer) resorted to it. Some of those teachers acted like autocrats, openly showing their likes and dislikes of certain students. Ruling with iron fists, they were determined to "sift the chaff from the wheat," as they used to call it. This rather oppressive scholastic atmosphere was, of course, not very conducive to fostering uninhibited overall development of talents and creativity, and quite a few students—the "chaff"—were made to resign from my school. As for having a little fun, there was no time and occasion for playing pranks on teachers. The few I remember, carefully planned to avoid getting caught, were selectively aimed at the old crammers.

Of the three institutions combining high school and junior college education for boys in the city of Mainz, the one I attended was the most elitist. It prided itself on the highest academic and educational standards among the three, and its students used to look down on the other two. In comparison to this scholastic law and order regimen, our *Jungvolk* meetings in Budenheim were sheer play and fun. After a couple of years, though, some younger teachers, most of them wounded in combat, were reassigned to schools at home. One of them inspired me to improve my math grade from a C to an A in less than a year. We had some of our role models back, and even though they were somewhat reserved at telling us about their front line experiences, we admired them almost like heroes.

I saw our old school principal, Dr. Schulze, only at official events, such as the beginning of a new school year or a national holiday. At these occasions, Dr. Schulze, standing on the second-floor balcony that was draped with a swastika flag, used to address his eight hundred or so scholastic peons lined up class-by-class in militarylike formation. But unlike the permanent presence of patriotic symbolism in American schools, there were no permanently displayed flags in German classrooms, no pledges of allegiance, no national anthem, and no ROTC-like pre-military training. This reflected German academic tradition which saw no place for such political symbolism in schools. However, God was permitted a place in the form of religious instruction, Protestant and Catholic, and the crucifix hung on the wall of every elementary classroom in predominantly Catholic areas. The Nazis did not change this tradition.

The mayor of our town had been elected in the mid-1930s. By Nazi decree he simultaneously had to represent the party's interests as well as administering to the town. He was a grandfatherly, gray-haired figure who possessed the rare diplomatic skill of balancing the community's interests with the party's demands. While I was not able to clearly discern between the two at the time, older people I talked to after the war told me that, in the long run, the mayor made the community's interests win out. They told me later about an isolated case of civil disobedience which the Gestapo from Mainz wanted to investigate.[10] The mayor talked them out of it, assuring them that he would handle the matter rigorously, and in the best interest of the Fatherland. He settled it somehow, and as far as I know, nobody was ever punished for political reasons, or sent to a concentration camp.

I did not become aware of the existence and horror of concentration camps until after the war. I learned that those who were aware of their existence kept their mouths shut, because it was a crime to leak any information about the camps. To assure total secrecy, the SS, Hitler's and Himmler's most devoted henchmen, were put in charge of these camps. Neither was I aware of the collective persecution of Jews as, to the best of my knowledge, there were only two half-Jews living in Budenheim, one owning a perfumery in Mainz, the other co-owning a tinware factory. Both of them could keep their businesses, and survived the war personally unscathed.[11] In retrospect, the way in which Nazi orders and directives were carried out in smaller communities depended largely on the personality and character of the local administrative authority, coupled with that authority's knowledge of predictable Nazi behaviour at county seats

H. Pfrengle's adoptive father, Dr. Otto Pfrengle, as a *Flak* communications corporal, 1939–40

and big cities, and the skill to steer a course of least obvious resistance with the local citizens' interests in mind.

The spring of 1944 saw a further reduction of per capita rations to about 1,100 calories per day; the black market was flourishing, and the local farmers had a heyday. By now, in addition to all foodstuffs and commodities mentioned earlier, practically anything needed to maintain even the most primitive lifestyles had become rationed: wood, soap, toothpaste, all clothing, sewing yarn, all household implements, and writing and toilet paper. Luckily, most newspapers were still in circulation and, cut into handy pieces, could be found in most private restrooms. It was always a good idea to carry an extra supply of sheets in one's own pocket. As for shoes, the average German citizen was allowed one new pair a year, or resoling of a used pair.

For the most part, this kind of rationing was an exercise in futility since most of the items were only available irregularly, or not at all. In the larger cities such as Mainz, the ration cards took on the role of a black market currency whose value could fluctuate daily as a function of supply and demand. This kind of activity was, of course, punishable by law, but the instinct of survival does not necessarily stop short of breaking the law. In the more rural areas, for example in Budenheim, bartering, a lesser demeanor than ration card trading but still punishable, was the prevailing mode of illegal exchange. As in any game of passive survival, the cardinal rule was not to get caught.

But true to the popular adage that necessity is the mother of invention, people came up with all sorts of practical ideas to ameliorate their plight. For example, stuffing crumpled newspapers between an overcoat's outer shell and inner lining helped to retain body heat in the winter, and I resoled a pair of worn shoes with strips of rubber from an old bicycle tire. The paper-stuffed overcoats made the starved people look fatter than they actually were, and I walked a little wobbly on my tire soles, but such makeshift ideas also fostered a sense of common sharing, and a certain sense of humor as well— an indispensable ingredient in any concept of survival.

It also saw intensification of Allied bombing. We had a close call when some medium-sized high-explosive bombs exploded about one hundred meters from my home.

Some incendiary bombs fell closer. One landed in a neighbor's backyard where, stuck obliquely in the ground, it could spew only part of its white phosphorous charge at an angle toward the neighbor's house. That substance was a really mean thing because it could not be put out with water. The only way to fight it was to suffocate it. With the air attack still going on around us, and working our way in the phosphorous spray's blind angle as closely to the infernal heat as we could tolerate, my father, I, and some neighborhood men and boys feverishly started throwing shovels full of dirt onto the white-hot, glaring volcano. My mother and other women brought sandbags and buckets of water. We used the water mostly to compact the shoveled dirt and sand, and to dump buckets over our heads for brief moments of relief from the hellish heat. It felt like ages before the small mound of dirt and sand covering the bomb began to block the phosphorous' forceful expansion, and it gradually turned into a hissing, steaming, and foul-smelling pile. The worst seemed over for us now. However, others weren't so lucky that day. Exhausted, and gasping for air, we took turns shoveling at a slower pace now. But from fire drills we knew that the bomb's incendiary charge could remain active for hours after the initial discharge, and we took turns guarding the fire pile. Our drills had been put to the test successfully, and I was proud of our neighborly teamwork. The scarcity of public firefighting equipment—for example, Budenheim had only one fire engine and a handful of volunteers—made such close communal collaboration an absolute necessity in the home front's war-fighting efforts.

Air-raid alarms became an almost daily exercise, but school in Mainz continued. When rail transportation was knocked out, I would walk the 10 kilometers home from school. Our *Jungvolk* activities consisted now mostly of helping bombing victims, and building wooden makeshift cottages for them. Allied fighter activity also increased, strafing any kind of traffic, even farmers plowing their fields.

There were some muffled rumors about an impending Allied landing in Northern France. But popular belief, fed by Nazi propaganda, held that an invasion was unlikely to come from an island like England. The reverse, a German invasion of the island, appeared more probable in the eyes of some grown-up observers. And after all, the pictures of the *Atlantikwall* we saw gave the impression of a solid line of heavy, seemingly impenetrable fortifications stretching from the Belgian coast all the way to the Bay of Biscay in Western France. But on June 6, 1944, the "unexpected" happened: "They came sneaking ashore on rubber soles." The *Wehrmachtsbericht* played down the landing (but on rubber soles they won the war, I thought to myself later). There was increased troop movement through our area, accompanied by intensified Allied bombing, especially of cities at the nodal points of rail traffic.[12]

We tuned our radio to the *Flak* air information network and listened to the location data for enemy aircraft in our area. This helped us to receive some advance warning of potential air strikes; the usual public warning by means of sirens often came too late, sometimes not at all. On a few occasions, we got to read Allied leaflets that tried to explain to the German population the hopelessness of continued resistance to the Allied advances on all fronts. This was in utter contrast to what Nazi propaganda told us. By law it was a crime against the Fatherland to read, discuss, or keep the leaflets, but a couple of times we secretly did it anyway. Was it really all true what we read there? Most likely it was factually true, but it was morally wrong to believe it. So, like most Germans, we still closed our eyes to that truth. And after all, weren't the secret German weapons we had heard about going to turn the course of the war around soon?

The *Sondermeldungen* (special radio reports, preceded by the sound of fanfares, announcing some German military feat) gradually ceased altogether. One of the last ones I recall was about Mussolini's "liberation" from a mountain top hideout in Northern Italy by German parachutist commandos under *Waffen*-SS Major Otto Skorzeny. The *Duce* had fled there after Italian Marshal Badoglio switched sides to join the Allies and assumed control of the Italian state and government. So Germany's staunchest ally had turned traitor. As for Germany's other ally, Japan, what we would sometimes hear through the grapevine about the war in the Pacific didn't sound good either.

The early summer of 1944 saw us *Jungvolk* picking potato bugs, according to Nazi propaganda another enemy weapon to defeat Germany, and air-dropped in order to devastate the German potato harvest. We also picked herbs for tea, dug trenches, and as a special service to the Fatherland, stole apples from the trees for soldiers who came through town. In August 1944, my school in Mainz was bombed out. I don't remember whether I was particularly sad or glad about it, given the circumstances under which we had been expected to acquire academic knowledge.

Chapter 3

Fortifying the "Invincible":
Hard Labor on the Siegfried Line

By the summer of 1944, a large part of the civilian infrastructure in the western regions of Germany had been destroyed or severely damaged by relentless Allied bombing. My high school in Mainz was bombed out in the latter part of August. Luckily the students were still on summer vacation. To me, it meant no more daily commute from the small suburban town of Budenheim on the Rhine River, including one hour of walking, 45 minutes of train rides, sometimes hours of waiting for a train, and sitting out air raids.

But if some of the students rejoiced at an extended vacation, the reprieve from academic toil took a quite unexpected turn: all able-bodied boys ages 14 to 16 (many of the 16 year olds were already pulling duty at anti-aircraft guns) were called up for sapping and entrenching work at the Siegfried Line. I had just turned 15, and felt a mix of pride, angst, and boy-scoutish adventurism. My mother, brought up in a rather authoritarian value system which she tried to impress on me, hastily stuffed some clothing and food in my backpack, my father gave me a manly handshake, and off we went by night train heading west to what we were told would become Germany's "invincible" defense line.

Our final destination, the town of Mettlach on the winding Saar River, located near the Dreilaendereck, where the borders of Germany, France, and Luxembourg meet, welcomed us appropriately with an air raid alarm, to which we were quite accustomed. But the sight of some enemy fighter planes doing their aerobatics in the clear morning sky brought a sigh of relief. At least no heavy bomber formations, spreading disaster and terror like in the big cities back home!

I wondered, though, about the absence of German anti-aircraft fire, or fighters, as the enemy aircraft were diving to altitudes of below three hundred meters to strafe road or rail traffic, a bridge, or almost anything that moved.

Having assessed this kind of enemy threat as manageable, or so we thought, we turned to inspecting our ground environment more closely. A huge Renaissance-style sandstone palace situated in a park by the Saar River, and belonging to the rich owner of the well-known Villeroy tile and porcelain-making

Nazi stamp of the *Buergermeister* as local police authority, Mettlach, in the vicinity where H. Pfrengle built fortifications for the Siegfried Line

company, was to be our home until the big German counteroffensive many people were saying would drive the enemy back, or so we believed in our patriotically romanticized youthful minds.

The inside of the rather luxurious palace quickly reduced our expectations to the reality of war. The roughly three hundred-square-foot room which I shared with nine of my buddies had a high, ornamented ceiling, a marble fireplace, a hardwood parquet floor, but no furniture; a layer of straw took the place of bunks. What the heck, if the Fatherland had called upon us to help defend it, no sacrifice seemed too big, not even sleeping on straw for a while. We dubbed our new quarters the "King's Stable."

The two thousand of us who came to this place (the military name for the Line was the *Westwall*) were organized under the auspices of the Hitler Youth, but our sapping and entrenchment mission was supervised by army personnel, mostly grandfathers physically unable or too old to serve on the front lines. Our basic equipment consisted of shovels, pickaxes, and hand saws. We were informed that we now came under martial law, and any attempt at desertion would be persecuted with the full force of the law. And no writing home, until further notice. All this made our feeling of self-respect surge; finally, the grownups were starting to treat us like their own. My parents should see me now! We quickly adapted to our daily routine: awakened at 6 a.m., wash up at a well or a small creek in the park, receive a combined breakfast/lunch ration of one pound of dark army bread (with traces of saw dust baked into it), two ounces of margarine (thanks to Napoleon who had it developed to feed his soldiers a cheap substitute for butter), two ounces of cheese or "Wurst," and a canteen filled with diluted *Ersatzkaffee*. Then we headed to our work site somewhere on the hills surrounding Mettlach, about an hour's walk, depending on the mood the enemy pilots were in at the time.

The scenic, hilly landscape around Mettlach, with its deep-cut valleys, was dotted with tactically placed heavy bunkers and pillboxes, with firing ports for heavy weapons and machine guns. Many of them had been built for the 1940 campaign against France, but the ones just recently completed were the heaviest ones. We marveled at their reinforced concrete walls, up to two yards thick, one-foot armor steel doors, hatches, and firing ports, telescopes, ammunition handling equipment, and the crew quarters with bunks (not straw!). The main mode of communication among the bunkers was by old-fashioned, hand-cranked telephones, though some of the pillboxes had their own power-generating system. Such a massive display of defensive strength impressed us a lot, and helped to boost our determination to do our part in this all-out patriotic rescue effort: digging and building an elaborate network of connecting trenches between pillboxes, bunkers, machine gun positions, and observation posts.[1]

The loamy and rocky soil made this a tough job. All the work was done by hand; machinery was not available (if it had been, the fuel for operating it probably would have been missing). The excavated material had to be spread evenly and camouflaged with sod and tree branches. After about two weeks, the blisters on our hands had calloused.

Digging continued, by order of the sector commander, also in rainy weather. Most of us didn't have raincoats or tarps (word had been we would get protective clothing when we reached our sector, but, as words went...). So we had to make do with the clothing we had brought from home. After some days of working in ankle-deep water in the trenches, our war-vintage boots disintegrated, and we were issued clogs with wooden soles. Until then I had seen them only on Russian POWs. My parents should see me like this! This footwear, or foot torture, which wore us, was useful mainly in developing new blisters, this time on our feet. As my friend Private Franz Frisch would say, this helped to establish symmetry of the extremities. For sure, having to wear them significantly diminished any thoughts of walking away from the line.

While the rainy weather kept the enemy aircraft away, it also made each shovel full of dirt twice as heavy, and working 8–10 hours, dripping wet and shivering, forced morale to sink to the point where some of my buddies decided they had done enough to ensure the Fatherland's survival for the day, and sought refuge from the rain in a pillbox. But they hadn't reckoned with the watchful eyes of our sector supervisors. A master sergeant or staff sergeant, with a head injury and sporting the *Ritterkreuz* (Knight's Cross), one of the highest German World War II decorations, dangling from his collar, furiously stormed into the pillbox entrance. When my buddies didn't come out right away, he pulled his pistol and fired into the bunker's interior. One boy got slightly wounded, the first ground combat casualty in our group.

Perhaps the trigger-happy hero wanted to set a deterring example, or take out his frustrations on the direction of the war, or perhaps his head injury made him flip out. In any event, during one of the twice-weekly morning roll calls we learned that two or three boys had "deserted" and managed to get back home. They would face court-martialing for their "treachery," and the same would go for refusing to obey an order, the grim-faced Hitler Youth leader impressed on us. "Understood? Heil Hitler!" He didn't like the muffled sound of our return salutes, and made us do laps around the park. His triumph of revenge, though, was cut short by the howl of the air-raid siren. There he stood for a moment, pale with rage, as we retreated into the buildings and shelters, with a sneering grin on our faces (and with no perceptible hostile feelings toward the Allied pilots, for the moment).

There were less disreputable ways of getting back home. One of the boys next door developed a severe case of intestinal disorder. A medic called "doctor" diagnosed dysentery, intestinal infection and fever, and because sick people were just a burden, the boy got shipped home on the next night train. Later, he confided in me that he had eaten soap.

H. Pfrengle, *tallest boy in back row,* with some of his *Jungvolk* group on an outing, 1942. *Fourth from left,* Gerhard Bockmeyer; *second from right,* Hans Batsch

The roll calls were our only official source of information. We heard about the heroic battles the Germans fought on the various fronts to stem the waves of plutocratic evil in the West, and bloodthirsty Bolshevism in the East. The shortening of the front lines, *Frontbegradigungen*, a favored German official term (meaning "retrograde corrections," or, more realistically, "retreats") came out as tactical successes, setting free forces to counterattack someplace else. Strangely, the new points of action moved closer and closer to the Reich's borders. As we were wondering about that, the pep talk focused on us, in our wood-soled clogs, as the "bearers of the nation's hope," "willing to sacrifice our lives for the *Fuehrer* and the Fatherland," "doing our best to make the *Westwall* impenetrable." We looked at each other, suppressing some unauthorized emotions in the face of what we saw, and heard, just from our local perspective confined to about 15 square kilometers of Siegfried Line.

Not a word was told us about the situation back home. I was worried about my parents; hadn't heard from them since I got here. The grapevine had some disturbing news about heavy bombing back home.

Sunny fall weather brought back enemy fighters and fighter-bombers. We learned pretty fast to identify, and respect, the *Thunderbolts* and *Mustangs* with American markings, as well as some British aircraft such as the *Spitfires*. Somewhat ironically, they made our lives less miserable, we felt, than the mud and the water-filled trenches during heavy rains. You could take cover from the aircraft, but not from the rain (as we had found out). I continued to wonder about the striking absence of German air defense. The official version was that air defense was concentrated where the real combat action was, not at our location roughly 20 kilometers behind the front line.

The grapevine, and our senses, told us there couldn't be much of a German air defense capability up front if enemy aircraft could fly all the way to our sector to play around so unabashedly, disrupting rear area movement and inflicting considerable damage to lines of communication. What unsettled my mind wasn't so much the absence of German air defense, for whatever reason, but the gradual realization that the truth was officially concealed. This was a big disappointment on the part of a young "comrade-in-arms" who wanted to be accepted as an adult. Such contradictory impressions and experiences of the last few weeks started triggering a state of mind I had hitherto been unfamiliar with: nagging skepticism about the adults called upon to fight the war, the kind of strategy they were using, and the kind of war the nation itself was behind.

Most of the pillboxes and bunkers in our sector had only a machine gun in them, some of them mounted coaxially with empty cradles for heavier weapons. "The heavy ones will come later," the one or two army granddads manning the bunkers would tell us, and ventured the vicious advice: "Why don't you go back to mother, boys!" (Much later I came to appreciate their courage and honesty.) At the time we felt shocked, not only because of this obvious lack of defense willingness on the part of adult soldiers, but in seeking male bonding it also hurt our sense of Fatherlandish identity. After all, we were trying hard, so we thought, to earn the right to put our lives on the line just like all those regulars (without knowing yet what this really involved, or meant, to fathers of families).

As to our questions about the actual combat crews to man the pillboxes and bunkers, we got the stereotypical reply: "Later." As my boy-scoutish mentality and patriotic romanticism began to painfully give way to a deepening cognition of war's realities, that evasive term "later" not only came to reflect a psychological escape

Westwall. Two-story concrete pillbox/bunker system, heavily overgrown with vegetation. Location: approximately three km from Mettlach; ca. October 1980
1. Concrete slabs of blown-up top story came to rest in oblique positions.
2. Concrete is camouflaged brown. 3. Firing ports blown open (bottom story).
4. Post-war danger sign

mechanism characteristic of the general German desultory mood conflicting openly with still unavowed defeat, but for the first time, rather nebulously, brought up the question in my mind: What would come *after* a possible German defeat? I mulled over the sarcasm in a conversation between some soldiers that I overheard: "Well, let's enjoy war while we can, because the peace will be horrible." Fear of an increasingly uncertain and gloomy future seemed to spread everywhere.

But those were forbidden thoughts for now. Current reality demanded a more practical approach to survival. By lunch time, we had already consumed our food rations. The fact that many farmers had evacuated the area made it easier for us to forage the fields, between the rows of dragon's teeth (pyramid-shaped antitank obstacles; see photo on page 50), for apples, potatoes, and beets. Baked over an open wood fire in the absence of enemy aircraft, such substitute for lunch became essential for our physical survival. Italian POWs working in our Siegfried Line sector had it much better. Although

Westwall. Concrete bunker, not destroyed/demolished.
Location: at Mettlach, on the Saar River bank; ca. October 1980

1. Manhole cover, escape hatch

they were taken prisoners by the Germans following the anti-Mussolini uprising by Marshal Badoglio in 1944, they still enjoyed a certain degree of protection by the Geneva Convention, which, among other things, meant they got a hot meal for lunch, while we did not.

Their uniforms and boots were in much better shape than the poor stuff we were wearing, and we voiced our disgust: "First we bailed them out in the Balkans, later in North Africa, then we had to rescue their *Duce*, and now they still are better off than we!" To be better lovers than fighters appeared to pay off after all, I mused with indignation.

The Italians worked on an antitank ditch stretching roughly one kilometer between two wooded hills. It was about five meters deep, with the slope on the enemy side roughly at 25 degrees, and 55 degrees on the opposite side. The Italians had done a neat job over some months, although we observed that they seemed to spend more time hiding from Allied aircraft than at their actual work site. Deep down I wondered whether Allied tankers were really so dumb as to drive their tanks into a ditch like this. Well, a sudden air strike a couple of days later seemed to eliminate that wondering thought. The Allies had cleverly waited until the work was completed, then bombed it. A couple of days later, about two hundred Italians were back to repair their antitank ditch. And then, it would get bombed again, I guessed. I came to realize that war had its very own game rules that seemed to escape the rational grasp, especially on the part of the defender.

We got our hot meal at supper, usually soup or some kind of diluted stew; and as we watched, the Hitler Youth girls in the kitchen would enrich leftovers with some more water so everybody could have a second helping. On weekends, we usually had a day off to clean ourselves, our quarters, repair our tools and clothing, and endure some Nazi indoctrination. If we weren't too tired we would find an hour or two to sing songs of a sentimental content, play harmonicas, shoot the breeze, or exchange grapevine information. There were rumors we would be relocated to the Hunsrueck Mountains, about 50 kilometers to the northeast, because the Allies had achieved an advance in front of our sector. The rumbling of artillery fire had, indeed, become louder, and when I asked one of our leaders about this, and contingency plans, he remarked in all honesty, it seemed to me, that the louder battle sounds had probably have to do with the shifting wind. Against my resolution to keep my calm under all conditions, until I would be absolutely sure, I lost my temper, and replied angrily: "It appears to me that the wind has shifted from your ass to your brain!" (If my parents had heard me like this!) Obviously, he was a low-ranking leader, otherwise I wouldn't have risked a tongue like this. He stared at me with mouth agape, and before he could say something I performed a hasty retreat. I came to wonder how much those leaders really believed in what they were told to preach.

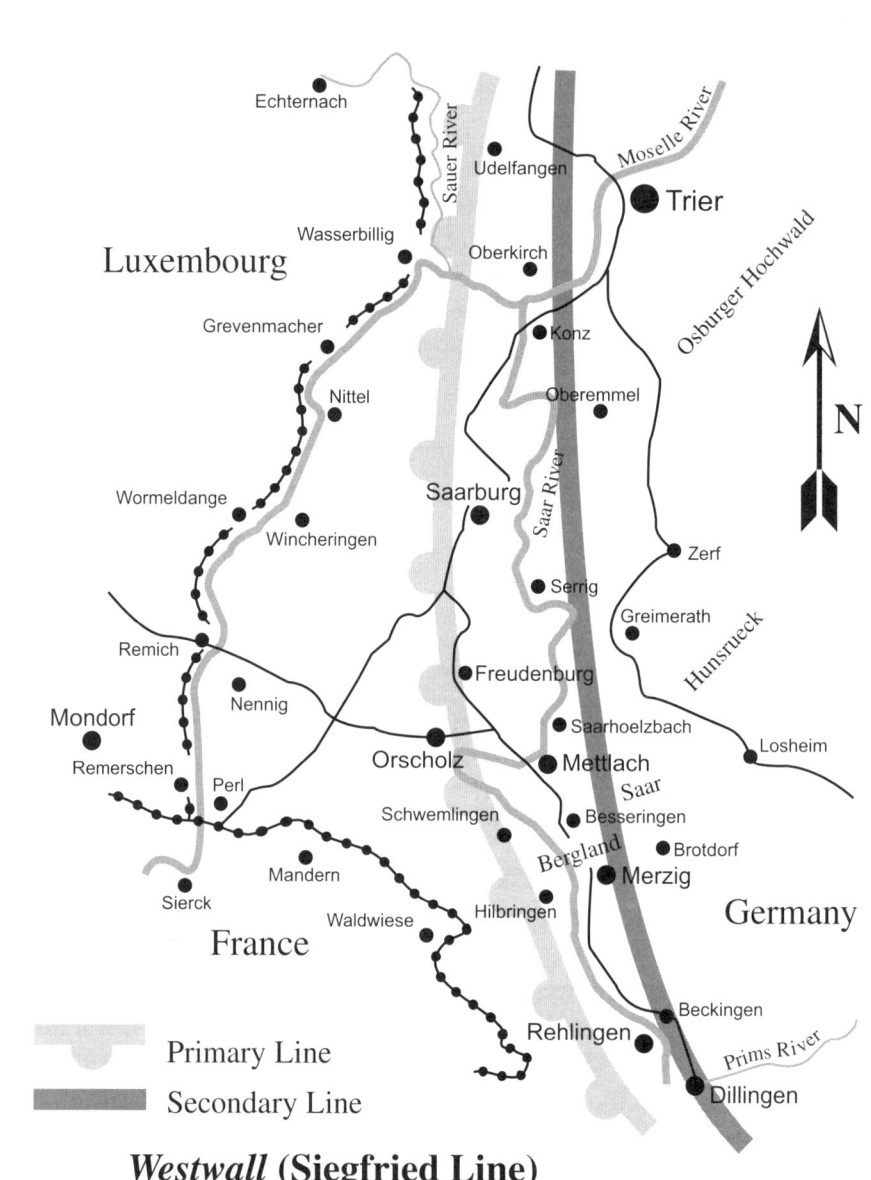

Echternach

Sauer River

Udelfangen

Moselle River

Trier

Wasserbillig

Luxembourg

Oberkirch

Osburger Hochwald

Grevenmacher

Konz

N

Nittel

Oberemmel

Wormeldange

Saarburg

Saar River

Zerf

Wincheringen

Serrig

Greimerath

Remich

Freudenburg

Hunsrueck

Mondorf

Nennig

Saarhoelzbach

Losheim

Remerschen

Orscholz

Mettlach

Perl

Saar

Schwemlingen

Besseringen

Brotdorf

Mandern

Bergland

Merzig

Sierck

Waldwiese

Hilbringen

Germany

France

Beckingen

Rehlingen

Prims River

Dillingen

Primary Line

Secondary Line

Westwall (Siegfried Line) Central Sector

Hermann O. Pfrengle helped construct
defenses around Mettlach

Sources: *Atlas of the Second World War* (Geographia);
     Atlas for the Second World War: Europe and the Mediterranean (West Point Military History Series);
     Across the Rhine (Time-Life Books);
     Road maps of Germany (Hermann O. Pfrengle's Collection)

With much of its population evacuated, the town of Mettlach was dead, offering nothing whatsoever in the way of relaxation or recreation, no movies to take our minds off the daily routine. In consolation, we asked ourselves who really wanted movies when war action provided so much more excitement: SS boss Heinrich Himmler's armored train came to town. We never saw him in person, but his armored train became a source of attraction for both our unit and Allied aircraft. As we were watching from a hill overlooking Mettlach and its railroad station, a

H. Pfrengle, ca. early 1945

cat-and-mouse game unfolded for three days, and went something like this: The train, representing formidable *Flak* power with about ten 20mm and 37mm-automatic anti-aircraft cannons, would engage enemy aircraft within reach. When a number of aircraft began to actively concentrate on the train as a target, it would simply retreat into the tunnel between Mettlach and Merzig.

After day one, Allied aircraft smartened up by placing bombs right at the tunnel's two entrances, thus trapping the train inside the tunnel. However, unbeknownst to the Allied aircraft, the Germans repaired the rail track damage overnight, and were ready for a new challenge the next day. On the second day, the Allied fighter-bombers managed to place some bombs around the tunnel's train side entrance, preventing the train from retreating into the tunnel. I marveled at the chesslike tactics. But if the pilots thought they had a sitting duck now, they were thoroughly mistaken. The train's automatic cannons spewed seemingly endless supplies of ammunition, down-ing two of them and keeping the others at a respectable distance. Now that was exciting *Flak* action as we boys had imagined it all along. Some low clouds came to the train's rescue, the aircraft disap-peared, and work crews started immediately to repair the rail dam-age. A few hours later, the train was back in the tunnel. The show was over for the day.

The next day brought clearing skies, and with it about 15 or 20 aircraft which appeared ready to repeat the day-one scenario. The difference in today's game was, though, that only about half the train ventured out the tunnel, with only about five cannons firing in short bursts, but still causing one enemy loss, as far as we could deter-mine. After a couple of its half-assed appearances the train retreated into the tunnel for good. Playing by the established rules, and as we figured would happen, the Allied players placed a number of bombs at both ends of the tunnel. This gave the train crew time to rest, or perhaps prepare for some more track repair.

Our anticipation of next day's act in this entertaining interna-tional contest was shattered, though, when we realized that one track had been repaired overnight, and the train had gone. I'm sure some of the Allied players in this cat-and-mouse game were as disappointed as we were at the time.

After Himmler's brief visit, the Allies again ruled the skies over our sector uncontestedly. When they came real close looking for tar-gets, we took cover quickly and avoided any movement, more by instinct than training. During the roughly 10 weeks there, our unit of 2,000 boys lost only about 40 casualties to enemy air action, we were told.

In a brief, but personally decisive change of scenery, I was des-ignated deputy leader of a detachment which was supposed to get some supplies from a rear supply point, shoe leather, among other things, pieces of which were needed for nailing to wooden soles to make more clogs. In addition to their blister-generating quality, the clogs had the distinct drawback of making our gait clumsy and slow-ing us down when running for cover. In making allowance for this disadvantage, we got used to seek cover earlier than with normal footwear, sometimes against the orders of superiors. We learned to voice objections like, "We don't want to get killed just because the

Fatherland won't give us nice boots like you are wearing!" Or, in a more correct common-sense way, we would mumble something about our duty to stay alive to fortify the line and preserve our combat potential for "later."

Our detachment caught rides on all kinds of vehicles, some of them running on wood gas which reduced normal speed by at least 50 percent and increased chances of becoming a sitting duck for enemy aircraft. But it felt good to rest our tired legs for a while. One of the soldiers in a car asked me whether I had been through basic training. I mentioned I had undergone air gun target range practice. He handed me an extra carbine "for shooting at enemy aircraft." When such an opportunity came a short while later, we jumped off the car and scrambled for nearby trees. He actually fired a few shots after the worst was over, and when I remarked on such a waste of ammunition, he said with a twinkle in his eye: "This is mainly for the morale effect."

At the supply point, most of the supply items we were supposed to pick up and bring back by truck were not ready; to get a truck would take a couple of days, perhaps. The small town an hour's walk away offered the first opportunity in weeks to spend money which we had brought from home (we didn't receive any pay for working on the Siegfried Line, but we could rest assured the Fatherland would thank us for our effort, we were told). After some unsuccessful tries, we finally found a vintner who, in strict confidence, was willing to sell us some bottles of local wine at an exorbitant price. If some of the readers should think now that we had a wild night on the town, I must disappoint them. Back at the supply point we traded the wine for a good and rich hot meal the likes of which we hadn't seen or tasted in many weeks. This culinary experience alone was worth the whole trip, I thought to myself.

Half the detachment, and its leader, stayed at the supply point while the other half, including myself, unfortunately, was ordered back. We shouldered some rolls of shoe leather, and caught a daylight train loaded with civilians and soldiers on home leave. Napping our way back west in a crowded compartment, reality abruptly caught up with us: the simultaneous noise of short automatic fire bursts, the shattering of window glass, a hard stop, the hissing of the damaged steam locomotive, and cries of people wounded made for a scene of complete panic. Somebody yelled "Out!"—probably the worst thing to do in this specific situation, because there were just fields and grassland on either side of the railroad tracks, bare of any cover. Against my survival instinct (to stay away from crowds) I followed the herd instinct, and ran, or rather clogged, across the open space toward a wooded area about eight hundred meters away. But now they came again: four or five *Mustangs* flying at an altitude of less than one hundred meters, strafing the crowd of perhaps five hundred people along both sides of the railroad tracks.[2]

I hid my face in the grass, my fingers clawed into the dirt, and I forced myself to briefly look up, just to see them approaching again, with the splatter of thousands of bullets impacting the ground, behind which followed the aircraft. A file of impacts was coming straight at me. I saw the muzzle flashes at the plane's wings. Now I must be dead, was all I could sense. I froze, unable to jump up and run again. I just stayed like this for the third or fourth sortie. The terror caused by fear of death had immobilized me. I don't know how long I stayed like this, perhaps seconds, or minutes. When the terror freeze started to give way to my returning senses, I checked my body and noted matter-of-factly that I had not been hit. My mind was still too numbed to feel anything beyond this realization. The first emotion I felt was rage—rage at a situation where I was exposed to complete defenselessness and passivity. If at least I had the carbine the soldier had handed me in the car, I would have felt better. In rational retrospect, of course, it probably was precisely this fear-triggered passivity that saved my life; and, of course, I should have taken cover under a railroad car; and in a later retrospect, what was the use of fighting a doggone war like this in which the enemy could demonstrate his superiority so overwhelmingly and cruely!

The cries and moans of the wounded reached my ear. Slowly I got up, shook the spattered dirt off my pants and noticed that the pilot must have turned slightly to the left, which made the spray from his outer right machine gun pass about a yard from my right leg. I looked around the "battlefield."[3] Many of the bodies lay still. Some were crawling. A bleeding woman staggered across the field, a small lifeless child in her arms.I started to tend to the nearby wounded, not knowing more about first aid than a boy scout does, and using dirty handkerchiefs, and strips torn from probably equally

Area of the Siegfried Line at the town of Mettlach on the Saar River. *Background,* headquarters of the Villeroy and Boch Ceramics Company, a former Benedictine abbey (about 260 years old then), where H. Pfrengle was quartered from August–October 1944, together with some two thousand boys, while working on the Line. *Foreground,* the bridge he crossed daily to his places of work, often strafed by Allied fighters dirty shirts and underwear for makeshift bandages. After what seemed hours (perhaps it was), helpers arrived, followed by a few ambulances and trucks. The less severely wounded were carted off on horse-drawn wagons. A young nurse told me to climb aboard one of them. As I refused, she insisted: "You are bleeding all over, go to the first-aid station!" There was, indeed, blood all over me, other people's blood....I still was too shell-shocked to curse this brutal slaughter.

The one thousand-year-old "Old Tower" in the park behind H. Pfrengle's quarters. In 1944, trees around it had been trimmed or cut to provide a better field of vision for the air sentry station on the tower's top floor.

My only other lasting remembrance from this "battlefield" was a German army officer staggering across a field, his right arm dangling from his shoulder by thin threads of fabric and skin, and insisting that he could walk to the rescue vehicles by himself.

Pondering this indiscriminate targeting of civilians and military alike, I later wondered whether that German officer would be eligible for the *Verwundetenabzeichen* (equivalent to the U.S. Purple Heart). This one-sided slaughter defied the neat military definition of "wounded in combat," where "combat" itself implied a situation where one wasn't only shot at, but also could shoot back and defend oneself as well. As a member of the *Wehrmacht* he most likely was eligible, including for veterans' benefits.

But what about the bleeding woman who held a lifeless child in her arms, and what about me for that matter, and the millions of civilians who also were daily "in the service of the Reich"? Well, we couldn't have been eligible for the preferential status afforded the military and ex-servicemen. "Quite unfair, even unjust," I reckoned.

Wouldn't this be food for thought by those who tended toward one-sided glorification of the military, and a condescending neglect of the civilian and nonmilitary majority of people who often were now being exposed to "combat action" at the home front more frequently than the military at a traditionally defined front line? All this in an increasingly brutalized war where we found the distinction between civilian and military had become blurred or extinguished altogether.

What about this whole business of a "just war" in which the internationally agreed rules of conduct, the Geneva Convention, were being violated so blatantly? Well, ultimately the victor would always claim his war was a "just" one, we boys concluded. "So let's keep on digging and do our share to help Germany win," one of my comrades seriously urged. "Yeah, but this would be a lot easier to do if they fed us as plentifully as the Italian lover boys over there," another added disgustedly.

All I can remember about the rest of this trip is that I could round up most of my buddies, making sure that two that had been, thank God, only lightly wounded got into medical hands, reaching the city of Saarlouis, and somehow returning to Mettlach. Whether we retrieved the rolls of shoe leather, I don't recall. Modern psychology would probably diagnose this memory void as an effect of "post-shock syndrome." Modern sociology might call it "initiation rite to death." My friend Franz Frisch, as I know him, would settle for "baptism by fire."

A couple more of my buddies found their way back after we had returned to Mettlach. We resumed the S.O.S.[4] routine of trench work, the only difference being that the shorter days of late October reduced our workdays to 6–7 hours. But then we received an unexpected morale booster. We suddenly heard roaring booms in the air, some dark objects were shooting low across the sky, too fast for aircraft but our instinctive reaction was: "Bombs! Take cover!" But no explosions followed, and as we looked up, we saw a couple of white contrails ascending at a steep angle in the sky; it happened again, irregularly, over the next few days. We were as flabbergasted as the soldiers around us. Information seeping through the grapevine had it that these were new German rockets fired from right behind our sector. Official confirmation followed, emphasizing that the V-2 was the most powerful, hitherto secret, weapon in the world. It would turn the course of the war to the Reich's strategic advantage, and, ultimately, to the *Endsieg* (final victory). We felt relief at the fact something active and important was being done. It was easier for us now to tolerate the daily presence of Allied aircraft, and the absence of German air defense, because Germany had something much more powerful in store.

But after a few days the V-2 activity behind our sector ceased. We were led to believe the launch sites had been relocated. Under the impact of that morale booster we worked a little faster, or was it the damp cold? They still wouldn't let us build fires in our quarters' grandiose fireplaces. I finally got word from my parents; thank God they were okay.

One day the story spread that a group of about one hundred boys working in the sector next to ours had captured an American wheeled armored reconnaissance vehicle and its crew. Apparently the Americans had gotten lost in a pocket of no-man's land, venturing too far ahead of their own line. The boys observed the vehicle approaching slowly at dusk along a sunken lane. While this may have made for good cover, it also was a natural trap which restricted the vehicle's movements forward or backward. Invisible to the vehicle the boys amassed at both sides behind the slopes along the lane. When it had stopped at a bend, and a crew member left it to crawl up a slope apparently to gain a better view of the terrain, howling hordes of *Jungvolk* boys descended upon the American intruders and took them by total surprise. Quick as lightning the boys swarmed all over the vehicle and, using a single rifle and their trenching tools' handles as weapons, forced its crew to surrender. Reportedly, nobody got seriously hurt in this surprise raid.

The secret of its success, we were told, was anticipation of the enemy's moves coupled with quantitatively superior surprise effect and the enemy's tactical weakness. But I took this "lesson" with a grain of salt; to me it was just a lucky coincidence, and it didn't inspire my thinking to play hero should a similar occasion arise. After all, what counted in the long run was qualitative and materiel superiority, as the Allies' advance amply demonstrated. In retrospect, could it also be that the American crew didn't want to shoot at youngsters? The young leader in charge of the surprise raid was decorated with the *Kriegsverdienstkreuz Erster Klasse* (Meritorious War Service Cross First Class). Years later, a friend of mine who also had been doing trenching work in a neighboring sector of the Siegfried Line at the time, confirmed that he had heard the story too, but was as unsure as I about its veracity. In any event, it was supposed to serve then as a morale booster.

The rumbling of artillery fire became louder, and traffic away from the front line picked up. Army trucks, some with wounded soldiers; half-track motorcycles; farmers with their families and some household belongings on horse-drawn wagons, with a cow, or two, tied to the back; staff cars; civilians and soldiers on bicycles; civilians with small carts—they all seemed to know where they were heading: east, away from the front-line, to the land of "later."

Off work we were restricted to our quarters, under the order of keeping outside contact to an absolute minimum. It became desperately clear, though, that the front line was moving in on us quickly. As the days grew shorter, and the weather worsened, Allied air activity over our sector sometimes ceased altogether. But when it cleared up, the aircraft pilots had their hands full. Occasionally, we were ordered to clear roads of wreckage in the wake of an Allied air strike. The new bridge across the Saar River in Mettlach received some anti-aircraft protection in the form of a 20mm quadruple-automatic cannon. However, this could not prevent the bridge from getting hit a couple of times by light bombs.

We heard that some concerned mothers had asked "the authorities" to have their sick boys sent home. I don't recall if this bore any fruit, other than causing trouble with "the authorities" back home. Rumor also had it we would exchange our shovels and pickaxes for small arms so that we could help defend our sector. But there were no regular army reinforcements visible here. The granddads in the bunkers became more surly and taciturn. Along with diminishing food supplies our morale reached a new low. The talk about the things that would come "later" to turn this gloomy situation around; the powerful V-2—when would all this come about? Our willingness to give it the benefit of the doubt shrank considerably.

From one day to the next, the front-line firing noise increased from phases of a more or less steady rumble to the discernible sounds of artillery and automatic weapons, the dry, sharp pop of tank guns, and other explosions. Flashes of light illuminated the horizon. The Allies had begun a local breakthrough.

Westwall (Siegfried Line) breached, March 1945

The next night we hastily boarded trains (the last ones to leave Mettlach, as I learned later) to take us home. The main station in Mainz fittingly welcomed us with an air-raid alarm. Herded into platform underpasses, we stood there like sardines in a can, so tight that the pressure waves of some heavy bombs exploding nearby made the crowd merely sway back and forth, as there was not enough room left to fall to the ground.

Rail traffic had been knocked out. Some of my buddies and I clogged our way back home to Budenheim, 10 kilometers downriver (westward) from Mainz. How good it felt to see my parents alive, our house undamaged, and to have my mother take care of the blisters on my feet.

The Fatherland showed its appreciation of our blisters and toil on the Siegfried Line by decorating us with the *Westwall-Ehrenzeichen*, a brownish- and white-striped medal ribbon which we boys were supposed to wear on our *Jungvolk* uniforms. But some of us, including myself, chose to wear it only occasionally, grudgingly remarking that a decent pair of boots would have made more sense as an expression of thanks.

Chapter 4

Bodies and Rubble:
Living with the Bombs

Back in the *Heimat* (homeland, Budenheim) by early November 1944, I indulged myself in all the amenities a home and a mother's care can offer: sleeping in a bed, eating potatoes and cabbage to make up for my weight loss, donning clean clothes and shoes without wooden soles. My buddies and I were relating our "war stories" with a sense of achievement, like old veterans. In our *Jungvolk* meetings the younger boys treated us with more respect. We felt more confident. The girls seemed to look at us with different eyes now. Wasn't there a glimmer of admiration and bashful desire—or so we fancied—in the glances with which they rewarded us? We basked in their glimpses of affection. The effects of our initiation rites were beginning to take hold.

But my good life didn't last for long. I had to yield my room at home to the commander of an *Eisenbahn-Baukompanie* (railroad construction company), a branch of the German Army Engineer Corps. The company was quartered in barracks about five kilometers downriver from Budenheim. As a commander, by military tradition he was entitled to special quarters and an orderly. Being from Vienna, he expanded his privileges into a lavish lifestyle of Austrian *savoir vivre*: Partying nights away, sleeping in until his orderly would come to remind him of some afternoon duties down in the barracks and made sure his commander looked spick-and-span as he climbed into his staff car. This commander, Lieutenant Loika, didn't quite fit my image of an officer. He used an inordinately voluminous amount of eau de cologne ("perhaps to camouflage the alcohol on his breath," my father remarked to me once), and our apartment was wafting from the smoke of his fancy cigarettes. He wore more than one ring on his soft, fleshy fingers, and always saluted my mother with a handkiss which, to my slight consternation, she didn't seem to dislike. An occasional small can of real coffee, or some other rare goody, helped to further endear him to her. My father called him "a gentleman of the old Austrian school."[1]

If many Germans had the frightful vision of eventually being condemned to die in this war, Lieutenant Loika demonstrated that, in the meantime, he could carve out a niche for living, and not the worst at that. As my friend Franz Frisch, himself an Austrian by birth, would probably paraphrase this philosophy of living in the face of impending disaster: "The Germans and the Prussians called a situation like that serious, but not hopeless; the Austrians used to call it hopeless, but not serious."

What was left of my good life took another twist to the brutal realities of war in that we boys were called up to dig out bodies dead and alive from the rubble left by heavy Allied bombings of Mainz and Frankfurt. A feeling of mental numbness returned as we brought them up and out, those still alive with expressions of horror, sheer pain, or utter incomprehension on their faces, others paralyzed by shock. They were evacuated to collection points where, in addition to aid and assistance, they were sometimes provided with Nazi pep talk, specifically how things would get better "soon," or maybe "later," but anyway better—slogans I had heard many times before.

But as before, I numbed my nagging thoughts in order to remain functional. During one of those rescue missions about December, I was buried alive myself in the caved-in basement of a building in Frankfurt. After a feeling of panic had subsided, and I was not injured, other than back pain from the blows of falling debris, my main concern became breathing. The dust was almost unbearable. Dimly recalling some survival instructions and the use of wet cloth, I urinated in my handkerchief and held it in front of my nose and mouth, fighting the instinctive urge to work my way out, and forced myself to wait in order to reduce my breathing effort, until the dust had settled, literally. Except for the sound of constantly collapsing debris, there was eerie silence around me, not a sound from the other people who had been in the basement together with me.

After what appeared to be several hours, and in fact was, I heard some knocking sounds from above. The rubble around me started to move again. I yelled, but there was no response other than those knocking sounds. Finally, I could hear the clanging of tools, sweet music to my ears, and yelling again, I received a distant response from voices above. I tried to protect my unhelmeted head with my hands as more debris came raining down on me. The voices came closer, then there was a shimmer of light through a crack in the rubble, and after a short while my rescuers had widened the crack enough to pull me out of my cave. How could I thank them? Well, if I felt up to it I could help them keep on digging, one of them said. I didn't feel up to that, but headed straight for a nearby water truck. Only once in my life (about six months later) did water taste better than there in Frankfurt.

When I got home my parents were waiting for me at the Budenheim train station, and I still remember the look of relief in their faces as they caught sight of me, unharmed, except for a few skin lacerations and an aching back. As I was a day late coming back, they had checked each of the few trains, with growing concern.[2] It felt good to be pampered for a couple of days. What surprised me a bit, though, was that my father made somehow sure I wouldn't have to go on another one of those rescue missions. I did not object.

My father had been called back from military service as a *Flak* communications corporal to his old chemical factory in 1940 to do "important" chemical research and development work that had a lot to do, as I remember, with finding food substitutes, pastes, and powders that would make for more or less terrible-tasting soups and mushy pap when mixed with water. Occasionally, my mother and I were the first guinea pigs that had to try out the stuff. After Allied aircraft had first dropped chaff, around 1943, to interfere with the 88mm *Flak* radiolocators[3] in the Mainz area, none of us knew what these thin metal foil strips with a layer of carbon paper on their backside were. People were told not to touch them (after all, the Allies had dropped fountain pens filled with explosive, and even potato bugs to destroy the potato harvest, according to Nazi information). My father was tasked to chemically analyze and examine the strips. He worked intensively for a couple of days, and then, with a slight trace of disappointment, but mostly relief, disclosed his findings: "aluminum foil." Now, I am sure that the chaff must have been dropped earlier elsewhere. Why the word hadn't gotten around to our area is one of the many examples of poor communication in wartime Germany. To the extent people bothered to put up a tree on Christmas, I later saw chaff decorate Christmas trees as tinsel, courtesy of the Allies.

Other nonexplosive items occasionally dropped by enemy aircraft and put to a utilitarian use by the people were empty supplemental fuel tanks mounted on the outside of aircraft to extend their operating range. Farmers converted these tanks into liquid manure containers—not to show their contempt for the enemy, but rather to enhance their "night-soil" fertilizing capacities. We boys found a more playful, less smelly use for the tanks by connecting two each of them with pieces of wood. On these pontoons we paddled along the banks of the Rhine in 1943.

Another of my father's important duties was to be the official "gas sniffer." In the event of an enemy gas attack he was supposed to run around the chemical factory, and if he smelled gas, trigger the gas alarm. While I was not aware of the absurdity of such an assignment at the time, my father must have been, and I am sure he had his own contingency plans (which, of course, he never talked about). Early on in the war, every civilian in our area had been issued a gas mask, the *Volksmaske* (people's mask). It was like a soccer ball's inner tube, the rubber enclosing the entire head so tightly, and hurting so much, that we skipped many of the prescribed gas drills. When, later, I expressed concern about the potential danger of my father's gas sniffer assignment, he told me not to worry because, at the speed the Allies were advancing, they would probably not have to resort to chemical warfare.

The Western Front kept moving indeed closer to home. The rumble of heavy artillery fire from an Allied breakthrough of the *Westwall* at Aachen about 80 miles northwest of Budenheim in early February 1945 was carried to our ears by westerly winds at night. Rumors had it that the Allies were "gonna hang out the washing on the Siegfried Line," where we had been digging trenches only a short while ago.[4] But German troop and equipment movements westerly, including tanks, on rail and roads started to pick up. Was this then the beginning of the big turnaround in a war which many had already thought lost? The German radio news mentioned the devastating effect the V-2s were having on the enemy, and London. Not until after the war did we learn that British fighters had become able to shoot down many of them before they could reach their targets.

New posters with Nazi appeals for the goal of *Endsieg* appeared at public places. Allied heavy bombing intensified, as did fighter activity. But something else was in the air, too, a tenseness like before a thunderstorm. Some people were whispering about a big German counteroffensive, others remained skeptical, or hopeless. We boys experienced a boost in our boy-scoutish imagination. Some tank crews heading west confided in us that they came straight from the Eastern Front where the Soviets had been halted, confirming what we had heard on the radio. Did the often-ridiculed *Frontbegradigungen* finally show the desired effect of freeing our forces there for employment at the Western Front?[5]

Frugal carbohydrate meals, sharing them with people who had lost all their belongings, and with soldiers moving through town, Allied bombings and strafings, complete blackouts at night—all this had become daily routine and made for a "normal" life style that I had become accustomed to. To keep people from bumping into each other in the dark, everybody was required to wear a small phosphorescent badge. With coal and firewood supplies dwindling or exhausted, the only place to get warm in the winter was at the kitchen stove. Nazi posters warned against stealing coal and cited names of people who had been caught and sentenced for having committed such a "crime against the people."[6] Coal, also called "black diamonds," climbed to a steep price in the black market which my family, and most other people, couldn't afford, or were unwilling to pay, either out of fear of getting caught, or out of a sense of patriotic responsibility. The latter, as a pure motive was, of course, a rare occurrence. Quite often, as in many similar wartime situations, the popular rationalization process would have it that people needed coal to cook meals for troops moving through town, or for evacuees.

Most of the month of December 1944 saw me and some of the boys doing paperwork to register people bombed out of their homes. They made the population of Budenheim surge by about 20 percent, without the immediate availability of adequate housing. We helped build makeshift wooden structures, assist in soup kitchens, and collect things to make those evacuees' miserable lives a little easier. My mother was pregnant, but that didn't keep her from sewing and patching together clothing for them. I remember how tired she often was, but she kept on toiling, as we all did, partly driven by a sense of gratefulness for having escaped those poor peoples' miserable fate—so far. A kind of community spirit had developed that made people pull together and share more as prospects for an end to the war without total destruction of the country became nil. My room of about 130 square feet was temporarily occupied by a family of four. Everybody contributed, and the farmers let go of some of their hoarded food supplies.[7]

Then came the *Fuehrer*'s "Christmas gift," the Ardennes offensive (Battle of the Bulge). According to the official German news, all hell had broken loose over the Allies on the Western Front. As this seemed to jibe with what seeped through the grapevine and what we had seen in the form of German troop movements, we boys began to take some new heart, hoping that this offensive would lead to a stabilization of the overall war situation and, ultimately, peace (even in official Nazi propaganda lingo the term *Endsieg* had lost its allure). Boisterous language, such as, "We will chase the Americans and English back into the Atlantic Ocean," had given way to hopes of sparing Germany the total destruction of its homeland and the death of hundreds of thousands more.

Radio broadcasts were again more frequently interrupted by *Sondermeldungen* (special announcements) about the rapid advance of German armor units, the capture of Allied supply points (which meant more of the desperately needed fuel), and thousands of Allied prisoners of war.[8] The daily *Wehrmachtsbericht* mentioned German breakthroughs deep into France and Belgium, supported by hundreds of German aircraft.[9] We figured this was the reason why we had seen practically no German aircraft in over a year or so: They had been cleverly saved for this decisive offensive! But after a couple of weeks, the *Wehrmachtsbericht* became less and less euphoric. When we heard about "heroic delaying action" by German forces, an expression that had accompanied previous German retreats, even we boys were able to translate it correctly: The "decisive offensive" had fizzled. The exhausted, war-weary faces of German soldiers coming through our town on their way back from the Western Front expressed disgust and hopelessness, and had a further demoralizing effect on the civilian population. "Now everything is lost," people whispered to each other, while the skeptics ventured an "I told you so." Spoken loudly or openly, this would, of course, have meant sedition, a crime.

Soon, some higher-ups had an idea for new "action" of my *Jungvolk* group's 13 and 14 year olds. We were to receive training in oar-propelled wooden cutters as part of contingency plans to evacuate military personnel and civilians across the Rhine. Cold weather notwithstanding, this brought a welcome change to our drab daily routine. In February 1945, we reported to the *Marine Seesportschule* (a navy sports training school) at the town of Eltville, across the river, where some mariners recovering from light combat injuries taught us how to tie knots, handle ropes and oars, and tell a cutter from a sloop. After they had assured us that we would never make old salts, and that this whole business was for the birds anyway, we began practice on the river, 12 boys to a cutter with a navy trainer at the helm.

The oar handles were definitely too big for our hands, but despite the blisters, and with the help of our trainers' cussing, we seemed to make some progress. One day, while rowing about one hundred meters off the bank, we heard a low-flying aircraft and, almost simultaneously, its machine guns, whose bullets formed rows of small fountains as they hit the water about 20 meters from our cutter. After a split-second of paralyzing shock everybody began to row desperately in the rhythm of his own fright. A couple of boys jumped into the water in sheer panic. But somehow, in all the confusion, we made it to shore unhurt. Above all, we were lucky the plane didn't return for a second strafing. Our faces were as pale as the trainer's who mumbled something like "That's it, no more," followed by some cursing. This marked the rather abrupt end of our maritime training stint.

For weeks in early 1945, following the failed German Ardennes offensive, many hundreds of *Wehrmacht* vehicles had been parked in the woods between Budenheim and the town of Gonsenheim, about four kilometers from where we lived. We boys inspected them, unencumbered by guards, or other security precautions. Weapons and personnel carriers, staff cars, trucks—they just sat there, practically invisible from the air, and with no military personnel around. Could this, perhaps, be an assembly area for another German counteroffensive? A low-level Allied air raid soon took care of the answer. Most of the vehicles were destroyed or damaged. It was precision bombing of a target area about two square kilometers in size. Even the bomb fuses had been set right in that most of the bombs detonated not upon impact with tree branches, but on the ground. The waves of concentrated detonations made our whole house shake. Some window panes cracked, but, again, we were spared the worst. Only a couple of heavy bombs, leaving craters five meters in depth, had fallen outside the narrow target area near our town.

But all this couldn't keep *Reichspropagandaminister* Joseph Goebbels from declaring over the radio Mainz a "fortress" which was ready to give the enemy a "hot welcome." He praised women who allegedly had poured boiling water onto advancing enemy soldiers as "heroines of the Fatherland." The thrust of his appeal to bravery was aimed at the people. It began to slowly dawn on us what he meant when he had declared "total warfare" back in 1943. As hard as we looked around us, we couldn't see any military preparations to make Mainz a fortress. We heard ironic comments that Goebbels may have been referring to the history of Mainz as a Roman fort two thousand years ago, or as a fortified city in the Middle Ages. New Nazi posters made clear, in no uncertain terms, that every civilian was expected to do his patriotic duty—or else. We followed orders, digging trenches and machine gun emplacements, and erecting obstacles. Farm tractors had to haul wooden logs for building tank obstacles. All this, we were told, was to make the *Wehrmacht*'s job easier. As to the *Wehrmacht* itself, it would come "later" to take up positions.

In an obvious and rather direct response to loudmouth Goebbels' bragging, Mainz suffered on February 27, 1945, the most destructive Allied air raid, which laid an additional 50 percent of the city in ruins and killed thousands of civilians. The raid was a total surprise in that it came from a solid low cloud cover, and in late afternoon. The sudden engine roar of hundreds of bombers descending on their target a few kilometers from our town made our house tremble, then rock, as thousands of bombs, whistling over our heads, detonated. Wave after wave they came, and, needless to say, there was no German *Flak* to speak of.

The ordeal seemed to last forever, and as night fell, the low cloud ceiling reflected the orange glow of the firestorm raging through the city. My father and I were called to help in rescue efforts, but since rail traffic had been knocked out too, we had to walk several kilometers, and when we got to the first burning city blocks the heat was too intense to do anything but assist evacuees who streamed out of the city. We didn't see any fire-fighting equipment, and water mains had been knocked out as well, most likely. In reality, there never was a "Fortress Mainz," and the Allied bombers had made clear in the most deadly way that there would never be one. Some front-line-hardened soldiers we encountered there said this was worse than fighting military battles on the ground.

Through our *Jungvolk* grapevine I heard that the morale of the Hitler Youth in Mainz was no longer what it used to be. There were rumors of a fight between a Hitler Youth leader and a high-ranking Nazi. Supposedly the youth leader refused to obey orders, and pistols were pulled. It is useful to interject here that membership in the Hitler Youth organizations did not automatically make one a member of the Nazi Party. Rather, membership was selectively followed by one or two years of service in the *Reichsarbeitsdienst* (Reich Labor Service). Following this service, young men were drafted into the *Wehrmacht*. One of my best hometown friends went through this cycle and never became, or was encouraged to become, a member of the Nazi Party.

Rumor also had it that the Hitler Youth band in Mainz was playing the "Tiger Rag," a cultural insult from the "decadent" West, at their secret midnight meetings. Such rebellious behavior was, of course, in stark violation of existing laws.[10] But if they could risk that on the higher level, why shouldn't we, on the lower rural *Jungvolk* level, also vent some of our frustrations, if not visibly, then in the form of a new bonding adventurism expressing itself musically? Seemingly out of nowhere songs like this popped up (literal English translation mine):

> On the sixth of June, shortly after midnight,
> sudden booms and muzzle flashes bright;
> Churchill yelled into the microphone:
> "Zap-zap, doodle-duddle, invasion!"
>
> Cargo gliders, parachutists
> and such other cunning things,
> carpet bombing, monotonously,
> zap-zap, doodle-duddle, invasion.

All men, old and small,
are getting drafted into the *Volkssturm;*
equipped with bazookas,
they throw everything away in the dirt.

In hindsight, this sort of black humor also served as a mechanism of escape to a psychological underground where we found some relief from experiencing all the absurdities around us, and ridiculing them. As our youthful identification with the Nazi regime was crumbling more and more, irony and sarcasm often took over as an attitude.

Chapter 5

A Call to Arms:
But Mostly Legs

Early on March 16, 1945, knocks on my home's window shutters woke me and when I opened them, there in the dawn stood our local *Jungvolk* leader in full decorative garb, accompanied by the local *Volkssturm* leader and a policeman. They ordered me, a 15 year old, to alert all of our 13- and 14-year-old members to pack their backpacks and report to an assembly point in Mainz. I rubbed the sleep out of my eyes and asked why.[1] They replied that American forces had rapidly advanced across the Hunsrueck Mountains during the last 24 hours and parachutists had landed near the town of Bingen, about 20 kilometers west of our town, a report later proven false. That was the last I saw of our *Jungvolk Fuehrer*. He shrewdly went into hiding thereafter.

I woke my parents to break the bad news. They didn't say a word at first, but I could sense their feeling of shock and fear. Then my mother, in her advanced state of pregnancy, began to have attacks of pain. My father tended to her while I packed my rucksack, and then notified the other boys. I didn't feel like leaving my parents, but since my father didn't tell me not to go (and he probably wouldn't have), I felt that "an order is an order." Good German upbringing, one can say. After all, that principle had been ingrained in me over the years by parents and state. It was the only concept of law and order I knew. We couldn't desert the Fatherland when it needed us more urgently than ever before. On a less idealistic plane, my father figured that we boys would probably have to dig trenches somewhere around Mainz, and we might have a chance to return home before too long.

Neither I nor my comrades were ever sworn into the *Wehrmacht* or *Volkssturm*. Our only pledge had been to the *Jungvolk*, not unlike a Boy Scout oath, which included a reference to acting for the well-being of the Fatherland and obeying orders of the authorities. These orders had the force of legal authority in the context then existing, vaguely called "emergency situations." The German concept of "authority" was entirely different then from what an American considers "proper authority" to be. When called, we went. My terms of duty on the *Westwall* in the fall of 1944, and from March to July 1945, were later recognized by the Federal Republic of Germany as "war service."

"We," that was a group of about 10 boys, began walking toward Mainz and taking cover occasionally from strafing aircraft. About halfway, one boy's father caught up with us on a bicycle to take his son back with him. Respect for the grownups kept us from interfering, but as the two of them retreated back home, we commented contemptuously on such cowardly behavior, and reinforced each other with strong words to desperately keep our morale up.

On either March 16 or 17, we proceeded to the other (east) side of the Rhine, just south of its confluence with the Main River. Several hundred boys our age from Mainz and surrounding area were combined into the "Hitler Youth Action Unit 117," which was posted over the area of several small towns. Some hours later, a *Volkssturm* chief declared that we came under his command, not the Hitler Youth's. The next day, some army officers inspected us, expressed dismay at the fact that we didn't have any weapons and were hardly ready for combat duty, and told us to keep ready for building field fortifications, because we would, from now on, receive our orders from the army. Such utter confusion in command channels and the ranks had a dejecting effect on our already waning morale. After all, we had moved to the "safe" side of the Rhine in expectation of a strong and organized defense effort to keep the enemy from crossing the river, Germany's most important natural western line of defense.[2] But the authorities here seemed as dazed and confused as we were. A medley of small *Wehrmacht*, *Volkssturm*, and Hitler Youth units were moving seemingly aimlessly back and forth across the area. I don't recall seeing any heavy weapons or tanks to speak of. Just a few kilometers to the west, American artillery was already pounding the Mainz area. Why wasn't our own artillery returning the fire from our side of the Rhine?[3]

We became not only discouraged, but disgusted, and I talked to my Budenheim comrades about trying to return home. Most of them felt the same way. The plan was that, together with two close friends of mine, I would reconnoiter a safe way to cross the Rhine by bridge or boat, and then, together we would work our way back to Budenheim. Once a way was found for crossing the river, one of the advance party would come back and get the rest of the group. We rehearsed the excuses for explaining absences, and I could rest assured there wouldn't be any squealers among my buddies.

Our advance party took off after nightfall on either March 18 or 19. We were familiar with the area and without problems reached the railroad bridge at Bischofsheim across the Main River east of the town of Kostheim. As we were climbing up the slope to the bridge, a voice yelled out of the dark, "Halt, or I'll shoot!" We told the soldier guarding the southern entrance to the bridge that we were on a supply mission. Thank God he didn't ask us for our marching orders, which we didn't have, of course. He let us pass with the request to let him know about supplies, especially wine, upon our return, or better yet, bring a bottle along with us. We told him we would try. Engaging the sentry on the other side of the bridge in a brief conversation about the situation along the Rhine, we learned, with sinking hearts, that the Rhine bridges had been blown up already some hours ago. So those were the loud booms we had heard! Once north of the Main, and with shrinking hope, we worked our way toward Mainz-Kastel, the only suburb of Mainz directly across from it. We got to within one kilometer of the Rhine when sudden American artillery barrages put an end to our reconnaissance trip.

Seeking cover, we crawled inside steel pipes stored in a factory yard. The clanging of shell fragments hitting the pipes produced an hour-long cacophony. Eventually, I dared peek outside and saw the western horizon lit with American artillery muzzle flashes. They were firing from the Hechtsheimer Hoehe hills just west of Mainz which provided tactical control of the Mainz basin. We were stuck, literally.

Locating and stealing a boat would have been too risky. The only way now to cross the river was by swimming it. To make that in the cold March waters over a distance of about one kilometer didn't seem very likely, but the main deterrent was that the Americans had advanced more rapidly than we had thought. They were probably already in control of the opposite bank and might have mistakenly fired at us as we reached it.[4] The door to going home was shut. We worked our way back; the sentry at the Main River bridge swallowed his disappointment that we didn't bring a bottle of wine, and back in our assembly area we felt relief that our absence hadn't raised any suspicions.

Some of my comrades had tears in their eyes as we told them that there was no way back home. They listened apathetically as I was trying to tell them that we had to stick together now, avoid any risky behavior, and see where, and how, we might improve our chances for a decent way out. I must have sounded like a Nazi propagandist, save for the content of my words. But, if I remember correctly, I also used that infamous "later"—a word I had come to mistrust—with its hollow ring of some hope in a distant future that eluded our imagination.

All of a sudden we heard combat noise at the southern flank of our area near Trebur. This was a rather shocking surprise as we had not been aware of any American river crossings in the Mainz sector.[5] A *Heer* (army), *Volkssturm,* or Hitler Youth type—I don't remember which—wanted to put us to work and picked me to take a look and see what was going on over there. I wound my way from cover to cover. Most of the intermittent firing seemed to come from an area perhaps a kilometer or two away. As I was crawling on my belly toward the edge of a wooded area to gain a better view, I felt a sudden, tremendous, deafening blast, a blinding flash, then darkness. When I came to after a while, the first thing I noticed was the foul smell of burnt explosive. My ears were still ringing from that blast, but I seemed to be all right. Right next to me was a small shallow crater, still smoldering. I was too scared to move and played dead for a while. When I finally looked up, I didn't see any combat action; there was just some distant small arms fire. My right leg began to feel strangely cool, and as I touched it, pieces of my pants came off, scorched by the explosion.

Gingerly and slowly I retreated on my belly into the woods. I don't know who had shot at me, and what type of weapon it was.

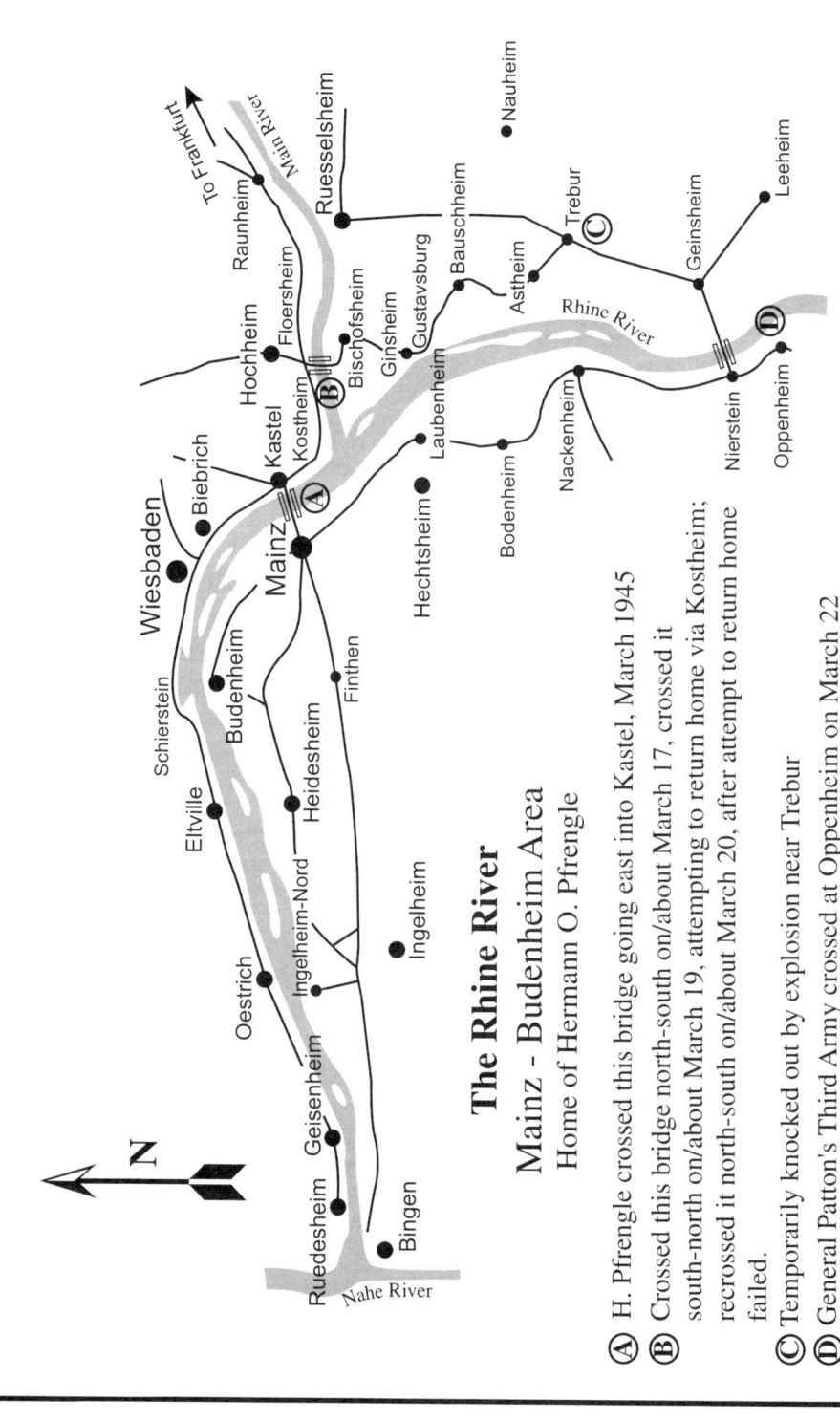

The Rhine River
Mainz - Budenheim Area
Home of Hermann O. Pfrengle

Ⓐ H. Pfrengle crossed this bridge going east into Kastel, March 1945

Ⓑ Crossed this bridge north-south on/about March 17, crossed it south-north on/about March 19, attempting to return home via Kostheim; recrossed it north-south on/about March 20, after attempt to return home failed.

Ⓒ Temporarily knocked out by explosion near Trebur

Ⓓ General Patton's Third Army crossed at Oppenheim on March 22

The fragments must have passed over my body. Perhaps it was only a stray round. All I know is that it was one of those miracles, letting me get away with just my pants scorched and my ears still ringing.

Returning to our assembly area I found everything in a turmoil. Nobody was interested anymore in the report of my scouting mission. In fact I had to scout around for several hours to catch up with my unit who were retreating, along with the whole medley of troops and civilians, easterly toward the city of Aschaffenburg. My buddies were glad to see me back, and I was glad also. They had even saved an extra ration of food for me, and we celebrated our reunion that night feasting to our hearts' content on *Kommissbrot* (the dark German soldier's staple shaped like a brick) and canned goodies. To my group, such rations were the exception rather than the rule.

At the small city of Babenhausen some efforts were under way to build up a line of defense, only to be discontinued when American artillery fire set in. An inhabitant of Babenhausen, which suffered casualties and damage, described the local situation immediately before the Americans' arrival: "I remember the march columns of boys moving through Main Street, with little enthusiasm (with a few exceptions). I also recall that many of the boys were killed or wounded...between March 23 and 25 in combat near Aschaffenburg; many ran for their lives...."[6] And run we boys, soldiers, and everyone else did—also called "relocation" in our orders.

In the squabble over whose command we would come under, it appeared that the *Wehrmacht* had won out. Our group was assigned an official leader, army Corporal Liese, who was in his late twenties. He had lost an arm in combat and was decorated with the Iron Cross First Class, and the *Verwundetenabzeichen in Silber* (wound badge similar to the U.S. Purple Heart). With Corporal Liese was a Red Cross nurse who pushed a bicycle loaded with their belongings. They both were friendly and caring. We boys were glad not only to have an officially assigned "guiding shepherd," but also a trained medic. They quickly gained our unreserved trust. It didn't take us long to find out that the two were lovers.

After escaping the fighting in the Babenhausen-Aschaffenburg area we were supposed to cross the Main River at the town of Seligenstadt. The ferry site there was under continuous aircraft strafing.

Thousands of Germans were trying to get across in all kinds of boats and floating contraptions. I saw one of them get hit, and the brother of a classmate of mine was swimming in the river still strapped to his backpack trying to reach the far bank. My classmate had told me that his brother carried Hitler's book *Mein Kampf* in his backpack; I do hope that the strength he must have derived from that baggage helped to save his life.

Two 20mm quadruple *Flak* cannons were untiringly spewing tracer rounds at the attacking fighters. Next to Himmler's armored train *Flak* at the *Westwall* some months ago, this was the most effective German light antiaircraft action I witnessed in all the war. When the fighters eased off some, our group crossed the river in a boat with, among others, the leader of "Hitler Youth Action Unit 117" at the oars. This rare and visibly effective demonstration of leadership not only surprised but impressed us, especially as he cracked some jokes which worked as a little morale booster. The only other time I had the honor of witnessing his leadership function was when, some days later, he instructed us how to pack our backpacks properly after we had been issued *Flakhelfer* uniforms and rucksacks in anticipation of *Flak* crew training.[7] The training itself was to take place in the Rhoen Mountains, about 120 kilometers northeast of Seligenstadt.

After our memorable Main River crossing, we began our retrograde movement in earnest and moved northeasterly through the narrow Spessart Mountain valleys which provided some reprieve from fighter strafing, leaving behind the noise of ground combat. As we received little official food rations, we had to live off the land by asking farmers for food. In the few cases when farmers or a local authority refused, Corporal Liese stepped in and requisitioned something to eat "by authority of the *Wehrmacht*." Usually, our requests were modest in kind: some potatoes, bread, turnips. We spent the nights in barns or sheds and haystacks out in the fields. The few times during the next couple of weeks that we took quarters in a school building or a gymnasium were a luxury. Another luxury was an occasional ride on temporarily requisitioned farm wagons pulled by horses, but this kind of luxury was limited to days when the cloud ceiling was low, and aircraft strafing was less likely. War-weary *Wehrmacht* soldiers shuffled along with us, but others went in the opposite direction, perhaps because their *Marschbefehl* hadn't caught up with the latest vagaries of the war.[8] *Wehrmacht* vehicles moved back and forth; many of the trucks had been converted to wood-gas operation giving off a sickening stench and clouds of wood smoke, which made for a good aircraft target marker.

Heading in the general direction of the Wildflecken *Wehrmacht* School and Training Area, where we were supposed to receive our *Flakhelfer* training, we left the protection of the Spessart Mountains behind and, in the open and rolling terrain, became again easier prey to strafing aircraft. How we were wishing for the day when we would have our *Flak* guns to shoot back at those bastards up there! The mere thought of it made us feel better already. During a strafing a boy from Mainz, hugging the roadside ditch next to me, wet his pants and, with tears on his ashen face, cried that he wanted to go home. I must admit that I felt less compassion and more contempt for him at the moment. I never saw him again, as far as I remember, but I do hope that he, too, made it home safely.

Our unit suffered a few casualties, but the Budenheim group was still intact. We were now moving in a northeastward direction, placing more distance between us and our homes every day. Because of the strafing, we switched our schedule and moved mostly at night. Artillery fire flashed across the night sky to the west and northwest. The explosions came closer. At that point, just southeast of the small city of Schluechtern, our orders were changed. Now we were supposed to support a new major defense effort, and our task was to act as scouts and messengers between army command posts which were short of communication equipment. Additionally, we were supposed to build field fortifications. This sounded like an old familiar routine we knew so well, more in theory than practice (except for our stint at the Siegfried Line the previous fall, and at Mainz some weeks ago).

We asked when and where we would receive small arms, equipment, tools—in other words, when would we be treated and recognized as real soldiers, and receive regular *Wehrmacht* rations? The hope of returning home was fading more and more, giving way to our desire for male bonding as a unit with some objective. We were tired of playing third-class warriors, we complained. Or were we? Corporal Liese explained, in an almost fatherly way, that it would take much more for us to become real soldiers, and that he hadn't earned his Iron Cross First Class overnight either. He also mentioned

something about legal age and the Geneva Convention which we
didn't understand, because if the *Wehrmacht*, or grownups, or who-
ever, expected us to perform duty for the Fatherland, as they did, we
should be treated like they were. Again the ominous "later," and
orders to report to various army command posts for individual as-
signments, put an end to our griping about "equal rights."

The new combat situation in our sector of the front near
Schluechtern is summarized in a German newspaper article:[9]

>...The German High Command tried desperately to halt,
>in particular, the advance of the 4th American Armored Divi-
>sion. A first attempt near the city of Bad Hersfeld had failed.
>Now a push from the Schluechtern-Freiensteinau area into the
>enemy's flank was supposed to at least delay his advance. The
>German attack force by the name of "Tank Training Combat
>Command Thuringia" was organized on March 25, 1945, from
>not fully trained reserve and replacement units and service
>school detachments, a total of about 2,000 men under the com-
>mand of Major General Oskar Munzel....

We hastily familiarized ourselves with the locations of the command posts, some of them in houses, others in the woods. The troops
were not much more familiar with the terrain and the details of the
area than we were. They were asking us questions about the Americans, their strength, equipment, and movements, which baffled us,
because we had hoped to get the answers from them. Sometimes,
the local civilian population had more information about the combat situation, and we relied heavily on their grapevine.

American artillery began to pound the area, and some of their
tanks accompanied by infantry appeared at a distance of about five
hundred meters, firing and disappearing. The messages we carried
back and forth seemed to say pretty much the same thing for the rest
of the sector whose front was shrunk to a width of perhaps 10 kilometers. The Americans were approaching carefully, but were able to
take a town. Nowhere did I see any heavy German weapons or tanks.
Small arms fire erupted at several points nearby. The lead content in
the air got pretty high, and we were glad we had been issued helmets
a day or two before. Also, our unit designation was changed to
Panzervernichtungsbrigade 13 (Tank Destruction Brigade 13), if I

remember correctly. Destruction with what? I wondered. But this question didn't bother me much as I was too busy staying alive.

In the afternoon I ran into some soldiers retreating from the line of fire. I asked them for their unit designation, and it turned out to be identical with the command post to which I was carrying a message. That had relocated, too, but they didn't know exactly whereto. This, and a sudden spray from a close-by American machine gun made clear to me that the German delaying effort was collapsing. For a split second I thought of hiding somewhere and surrendering to the Americans. But what would my buddies think of me later? That was important to me. I turned around and helped drag some of the wounded to the nearest houses, and may not have returned the undelivered message. All I wanted now was to reunite with my comrades.

Here is Major General Oskar Munzel's account of that defensive and delaying effort and German fighting power:[10]

> My Combat Command was entirely without artillery, anti-tank guns, communications, supply units. My small command post was mobile, but was equipped only with the bare essentials....Only the detachments who had come from the Service School in Wildflecken were combat-ready. Their personnel consisted of elderly sergeants and non-commissioned trainees of the Army Field Forces. The other units had only a few officers and NCO's; their bulk was made up of very young recruits who had not yet completed their training. The equipment consisted only of light infantry weapons, including some man-portable antitank weapons. There were only a few combat vehicles...field ranges and supply and support vehicles; these were mostly wood-gas-powered, as had been common in the army replacement units for a long time....The two Armored Infantry Battalions were combined into a regiment under the command of Major Schilling. The *Flak* units were also organized into a regiment of two battalions (the former *Flak* Brigade had one single anti-aircraft gun left)....
>
> On March 29, the...Combat Command Thuringia received orders to occupy a sector facing west [see General Munzel's map on page 73]. Because of the sector width...the only way to do this was by means of strong point-like security positions. This

was accomplished without enemy contact. The tank destroyer company, which was almost out of fuel, was initially assigned a mobile reserve mission, next to local infantry reserve units in the subsectors to the right. Communication between the various units was maintained by liaison officers and liaison NCO's, and utilizing the local civilian telephone net.[11] There was telephone connection with the 7th Army Headquarters. Some officers and approximately 150 men were assigned as security force for the town of Schluechtern. Also, there was a small unit of about 50 men in the town of Flieden.[12]

In the afternoon of the 30th, I received by phone the personal order from the Supreme Commander of the 7th Army to attack, with the available tanks, the right flank of a strong American armor force which was advancing from the west of the Vogelsberg Mountain Range toward the city of Kassel....I pointed out to him that chances...for success were low in view of the fact that only a few tank-destroyer tanks were available to me, and radio communication was nonexistent—the only way for me to direct the attack would have been from my staff car, or on foot...also, fuel supplies hadn't arrived yet. However, as nothing else was available at the moment, and the objective of gaining time to build up a new front was of decisive importance, the Supreme Commander insisted that his orders be carried out. I decided not to pull back the sector's security forces in order to maintain a readily available basis for counter-attacks close to the enemy line....When I arrived in the early morning at the forward-most observation post at the sector's right wing, only some enemy wheeled vehicles were visible, moving along his east-bound route of advance.

...On my way to the sector's center (*Flak* Regiment), I was about to enter the town of Gunzenau in my small cross-country staff car when I saw at a distance of about 200 meters...a column of American tanks with mounted infantry advance to the east....This meant that the *Flak* peoples' security position had already been penetrated....As they didn't notice me I was able to retreat quickly. I intended to alert headquarters and other units as fast as possible, something that normally could have been done in no time...using the command radio net. But under the

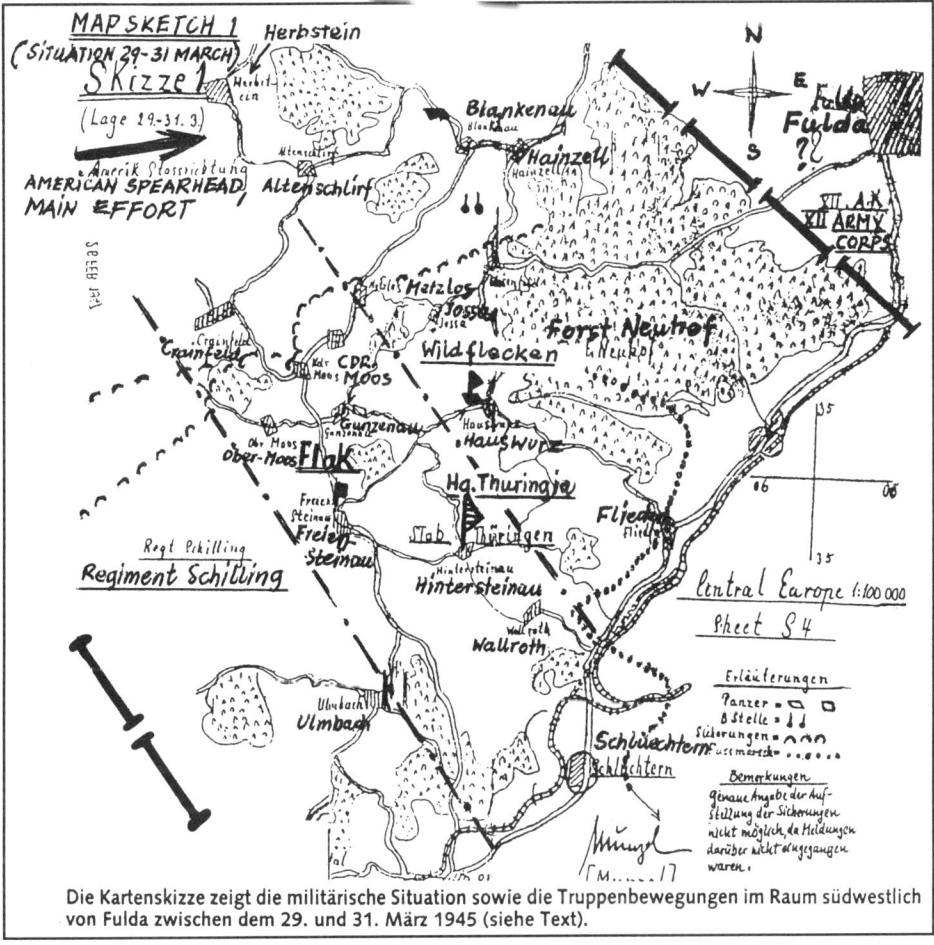

Die Kartenskizze zeigt die militärische Situation sowie die Truppenbewegungen im Raum südwestlich von Fulda zwischen dem 29. und 31. März 1945 (siehe Text).

The map sketch shows the military situation and troop movements in the area south-west of Fulda during the period 29–31 March 1945 (see text).

Translation of notations in lower right corner of General Munzel's map sketch

Central Europe 1:100,000
Sheet S4

Explanations:
Tank(s): ⬭
Observation Post: ♦♦
Tactical Security Forces: ∩∩ ∩∩
Foot march: ....

Indication of Tactical Security Forces' precise positions is not possible, because reports/messages about them had not come in.

⊢──────⊣ indicates the northeastern and southeastern boundaries of Combat Command Thuringia's sector; the sector was about 25 km long and 10 km deep, at the onset of engagement, but quickly shrank thereafter.

──·── indicates boundaries between CC Thuringia's

(⊢ Headquarters Command Post) three major force components:

Regiment Schilling;

Flak (⌐);

"Wildflecken" (⌐) (units from the nearby Wildflecken Army School).

Fuldaer Zeitung

existing conditions, time was lost. When I reached the next security company, I already heard tank fire from the Hauswurz area, location of the Wildflecken Service School and tank-destroyer command posts. Later, I learned that the tanks were destroyed with almost no resistance, while refueling in the town.[13] They were unable to lay their guns from the low-lying town at the enemy tanks positioned on the higher terrain (the disadvantage of the tank-destroyer vis-a-vis the tank with a rotating turret).

Returning directly wasn't possible any longer. So I tried to get through the expansive forest area south of Fulda—Forst Neuhof; after a couple of hundred meters I had to leave my car behind because of engine trouble. After a 30 kilometer cross-country walk...together with my aide and driver, I reached the command post which had pulled back to the town of Weiperz. My Chief of Staff had correctly ordered a withdrawal to the line Flieden—Schluechtern—Bad Soden....The enemy's tanks and infantry followed only hesitantly, and accompanied by constant air observation. The Wildflecken Battalion had been initially scattered, and of the *Flak* people only about 700 or 800 came back. We succeeded during the two Easter Holidays (April 1 and 2), when combat activity was low, to establish a new front line by taking back the main line of resistance to the mountains southeast of the Kinzig River, in connection with a shortening of the front line, and in order to prevent destruction of the towns located in the Kinzig valley by enemy air attacks and street fighting.

Thus ended the German counterpush intended in this area of Upper Hesse, as was to be expected in the situation described by General Munzel. It was blown apart by the Americans before it could materialize, like so many times before, and a few times thereafter.

This was how we had spent the 1945 Easter holidays, about two weeks after leaving our hometown of Budenheim. I remember them vividly also for freshly baked Easter pie which some good-hearted farm women handed us. We wondered how our families back home were doing: were they still alive? But there was no time left for musing over questions like these. We had to remain functional. Survival had become the paramount instinct, and we could control it only so far.

As an afterthought, I couldn't make sense of General Munzel's Combat Command designation as "Tank Training" and "Thuringia." The units certainly didn't have anything to do with tank training; there were no tanks save for the few tank-destroyers, and none of the units came from Thuringia. The only explanation I can find for such strange designations is that they were meant to confuse enemy intelligence. This might also explain why our unit designation had been changed to "Tank Destruction Brigade 13" at the same time. Perhaps, the misleading verbal emphasis on "tank" was to trick the enemy into believing that there was a whole bunch of tanks and antitank capabilities confronting him. While this explanation may run the risk of insulting American intelligence, it would have fit the desperate German mind-set at the time. Perhaps another rationale is that it reflected wishful thinking perpetuated to respond to Hitler's outlandish dreams and constant demands for action.

Our unit had suffered a few minor casualties in this Upper Hesse adventure, but our Budenheim hometown group escaped unscathed. Now we knew that the *Flakhelfer* training at Wildflecken, which we had been looking forward to so much more than message running or foxhole digging, was out due to the absence of anti-aircraft guns. But as a consolation prize we had at least been issued the bluish *Luftwaffe* (air force) uniforms and rucksacks, a most welcomed improvement over our *Jungvolk* uniforms and flimsy homemade backpacks.[14] The new stuff really came in handy in the cold nights up here in the Rhoen Mountains. I was also glad to get rid of the worn-out civilian trousers which had taken the place of my burnt pants about a week ago, or so. Corporal Liese informed us that "Americans permitting," we were heading toward the Hammelburg Infantry Training Center where we would receive training in antitank close-in defense. So, early April saw us moving eastward, true to the motto "a call to arms—but mostly legs," though we began to tire of this constant calling, and our equally confused legs too.

Some of the towns and villages we moved through had already hung out white flags from church steeples and houses to signal surrender to the Americans hard on our heels. I felt dejection, no longer because of a "display of cowardice," but rather because these white bed sheets symbolized a resolve that I and my buddies were lacking. These simple and friendly village folks defied the Nazi order to fight to the "last drop of blood," risking a charge of treason, and its consequences. Yet they seemed to know what they were doing while we did not. Deep down I somehow envied them for their perception that their town was part of the Fatherland, and by saving their homes from destruction they would also help save the Fatherland, as some of the locals explained to us. I dimly recalled some similar reasoning of my father's. My thoughts began to wander off. How were my parents living under American control—if they were still alive? And my mother in her pregnancy? But the approaching combat noise drowned out such feelings and musings. The "here and now" pushed the concept of "home" into the abstract.

Almost needless to say, we never made it to the Hammelburg Training Center. The Americans were faster. Instead we moved southeasterly now via the towns of Mellrichstadt and Roemhild toward the city of Coburg. Corporal Liese told us we would receive *Flakhelfer* training in that area. We also heard that the American advance had finally been halted.[15] Combat noise had subsided in the distance, except for the ubiquitous fighter strafings. A particularly severe attack injured or killed most of the horses, and some men, of a horse-drawn field artillery unit. Local butchers turned the horse meat into smoked sausages, a welcomed addition to our usual protein-poor food. We lived on horse sausage for days until the sight and taste of it made me sick.

Corporal Liese's companion, the nurse, kept dutifully pushing their bicycle, but lately we saw an occasional tear in her eyes. She had covered about four hundred kilometers together with us, and although she stayed somewhat aloof from us, she had a friendly word for us now and then. We came to like her very much. One day, Liese turned over the command of our group to me and said he would be back the next day. He and the nurse disappeared, and when he returned alone, he told us she was ill, and he had to leave her behind with friends who lived nearby. We felt a real loss. She had administered first aid to many wounded along our trek's route. Being regarded as something like a mother figure, she gave us a feeling of some security, and being cared for. "Just make sure nobody gets wounded from now on," the corporal warned us. As for any other possibilities, we would make damn sure that survival remained the name of the game.

As we came closer to the small city of Sonneberg, the rumble of artillery fire picked up again, this time not from the west, but the south. The *Luftwaffe* facility where we were supposed to receive *Flakhelfer* training was in the process of being dissolved. There were no *Flak* guns left; however, there was something else that caught our immediate attention: a *Luftwaffe* depot warehouse. We wanted to see what they had in store! A guard stopped us, warning that the depot will be blown up shortly, but Corporal Liese pulled his rank, and we rushed inside, where we found other scavengers, including civilians, at work. Our eyes popped out at the sight of all the goodies. This was better than guns. We sneaked out a different route, with new boots, leather "bomber" jackets, paratrooper knives, and cans of high-energy chocolate prepared for aircraft crews. We would have loved to also trade our rotten foot rags for new socks, but couldn't find any in the rush. As we heard the warning whistles, and the first demolition charges went off, we left the scene with a feeling of accomplishment, and fury over the idiocy of blowing up all those goodies. Why not let at least the refugees who had lost everything have some of the stuff? Because "an order is an order."

Our immediate order was to help defend Sonneberg. Corporal Liese was called to a meeting with the post commander to find out how we were to accomplish that with rifles, pickaxes, or shovels. The following eyewitness accounts give—better than I can—a more complete picture of the last couple of days of fighting in and around Sonneberg:

> The Third U.S. Army under the command of Lieutenant General George Patton carried its irresistible push toward Coburg and Sonneberg....On April 9 and 10, the end of the "Thousand Year Reich" was near in the Sonneberg area: Strafing aircraft set the storage buildings around the railroad station ablaze; locomotives, freight cars and tracks were severely damaged. American artillery and tanks fired on the nearby villages of Mupperg, Rauenstein, Theuern and Bachfeld...causing extensive damage and casualties....Colonel Baumeier, the Sonneberg post commander, apparently thought he could halt the American advance by bringing the *Volkssturm*—15 and 16 year-old Hitler Youth boys, veterans and pensioners—into action. Tank obstacles were hastily erected. He was killed defending one of

these....Allied aircraft dropped leaflets demanding the city's un-conditional surrender. On April 10, people stormed the *Luftwaffe* depot at Woolworth and Kresge, where millions of *Reichsmarks* worth of high-quality clothing (and personal equipment items) were stored....Despite several interventions by citizens the *Wehrmacht* blew up the Woolworth building by means of demolition charges....Mobile court-martial detach-ments unfolded their terror activities....They killed a young sol-dier who tried to survive the war...another one was killed by military police....

The *Wehrmacht* also blew up one span of the railroad bridge....This militarily senseless act made it difficult to get vi-tal supplies to the city's population in the months after the war....Simultaneously, Sonneberg became the target of Ameri-can artillery firing from the Effelder area, causing additional damage....White flags...announced Sonneberg's surrender...on April 12....[16]

The last German "soldiers" we saw was a group of 10 to 12 year-olds...who, together with their trainer, were running along the road at Huettensteinach (a suburb)....The U.S. Army was firing across the village....We heard machine gun fire from the railroad tracks, and the whistle of a locomotive. Presumably members of a German demolition detachment were trying to escape by means of a locomotive. But a U.S. jeep-mounted machine gun frustrated the attempt....The engineer was killed. The others escaped uphill into the woods....Then a jeep with a machine gun appeared in our street, followed by two tanks and a convoy of trucks....They took quarters at "Vick's Inn" around 6 p.m., April 12....[17]

On April 10, trees were dynamited to form tank obstacles along route F-281....U.S. advance parties moved into the town of Friedrichshoehe, where a U.S. officer was killed. At the time *Waffen*-SS was positioned near the Siegmundsburg cemetery. The next day, scattered groups of *Wehrmacht* soldiers were seen in Siegmundsburg. An American artillery observer plane circled over the town. During the day U.S. tanks fired into it from their positions at Friedrichshoehe. *Wehrmacht* and *Waffen*-SS suf-fered casualties. Around 4 p.m. U.S. infantry, accompanied by tracked vehicles, captured Siegmundsburg. They took over the houses, and the civilian population was quartered in three inns. The same evening U.S. troops opened fire on the town of Neuhaus where no white flag had been flown. The pounding did not cease until around 3:30 p.m., April 12....When we were later permitted to return to our houses we noticed what seemed to be a blatant abuse of our beloved German potatoes: Potatoes scattered everywhere from which strange, square-shaped and long portions had been punched out. Our kitchen stove was one greasy, sticky mess....Much later we learned that this was a new way of preparing potatoes which would sweep in a triumphal march all over Europe under the name of "french fries."[18]

As SS had taken down the capitulation flag, U.S. tanks opened fire with incendiary rounds, followed by high-explosives, on the town of Theuern on April 12. Many houses, and the church, burned down...others were badly damaged....In the lower part of town, German sharpshooters killed two U.S. infantry men, whereupon U.S. tanks, firing from the upper part of town, destroyed more of its lower part....After Theuern was completely in U.S. hands, American soldiers helped the local people fighting house fires....[19]

Some of the above descriptions bring back memories long buried under the trash heap of history, adding to those which have remained, such as carrying small arms ammunition to German machine gun positions around Sonneberg; dodging American infantry and artillery fire; reporting to a supply point in a basement to be issued small arms, just to see there weren't any left for us; catching sight of a couple of *Volkssturm* men throwing their rifles into a stream; Corporal Liese arguing with a *Waffen*-SS member; and barely avoiding capture, or worse, by Americans who were just a block away.

We made a "tactical retreat" into the Thueringer Wald mountain range north of Sonneberg, continuing as usual on foot. Food supply became a problem again. Usually, the first order of the day was to find something to eat in the nearest village. Warm meals were the exception. At one army supply point we received a half pound of margarine apiece, but nothing to go with it, and I subsequently developed a long-lasting aversion to the blubbery stuff. But more than once were we turned away from military field kitchens, and told to find food somewhere else, according to the widespread motto "everybody for himself." Not even our good Corporal Liese could help. We sensed how much he missed his nurse companion, and we took daily turns helping him with chores and things which required two arms.

The Americans were not on our heels anymore, and we wound our way in a leisurely fashion through the Frankenwald mountain range to the town of Naila, about 10 kilometers west of the city of Hof. Naila became an assembly area for another medley of the Fatherland's last warriors. There must have been thousands of them. *Waffen*-SS became more numerous too, eyeing us critically. Discipline became tighter. Corporal Liese wanted us to clean his boots daily. Our food situation improved. We received word that we came under a new command, and things would change from now on. We were to be part of a new German counteroffensive, as some crack officers told us in pep speeches. Well, we had heard and experienced that dream talk before. The reactions among our group were swinging between sarcasm and some renewed hope, and seemed to settle at a let's-wait-and-see attitude.

Along with a decrease in enemy artillery and air activity in those mid-April days, we could sense a change of affairs that seemed to be in the mild spring air. We were issued civilian bicycles (probably requisitioned like my own bike last year). About two hundred of us pedalled the roughly 50 kilometers to an army depot at the city of Plauen, northeast of Hof, to pick up small arms. With brand-new automatic assault rifles *(Sturmgewehr 44)*, antitank grenade launchers *(Panzerfaust)*, and pistols strapped to our bikes and bodies, we came back with enough weapons to equip a whole battalion.

The next couple of days saw us doing target practice, another step towards male bonding and feeling more manly, I guess, and the superficial feeling of satisfaction at being found worthy to carry weapons. In retrospect, it was part of the fulfillment of our boy-scoutish dreams, but we lacked the personal determination to kill. "Kill not even an enemy?" we asked each other one night, as our Budenheim clique was discussing the consequences of our new status as bearers of arms. Some were willing to kill in a case of immediate self-defense but not "in general." But where to draw the line in war? Others were undecided. It was obvious that in our psychological development we hadn't yet reached the "mature" state of mind expected of a soldier. Bearing arms was one thing, using them to kill was another. We left it at that for the time being.

We had soon used up the sparse supply of practice ammunition. One of the boys in a neighboring unit got killed while practice-firing an antitank grenade launcher. American air and artillery activity started to pick up again. Much to our surprise, there was some German artillery response. Our rite of passage in the form of getting acquainted with the use of the new automatic assault rifles was short-lived: we had to turn them over to a regular army unit but didn't receive their old K-98 (a model of the 1898 carbine) in exchange. In my recollection, the lack of ammunition rendered useless many weapons, new and old. We were allowed to keep the P-38 pistols with one or two magazines. This momentarily relieved us somewhat of having to come to terms with soldierly expectations.

Our next destination was the city of Selb, about 50 kilometers east of Naila, and five kilometers from the Czech border. We were quartered in an old school building with thick walls, where we rested for a couple of days, also courtesy of fighter strafing and occasional light artillery fire which kept us inside. Piling students' desks inside the classroom windows provided some protection against flying glass and fragments. We hadn't felt that safe in a long time. Around Selb there was the familiar scene of confusion: remnants of German units asking for directions, a desolate stream of refugees on horse wagons, or on foot, and the *Waffen*-SS acting as if the "final victory" was near (well, in a way, it was). Corporal Liese brought the new orders for our group: we would be at the disposal of local army headquarters, primarily as messengers, scouts, and ammunition haulers, an exercise we had been through several times already, the last time about a week ago and one hundred kilometers west of here.

But this time our bicycles added the additional benefit of making us more mobile. Mission briefings and familiarization with unit designations and positions alternated with trips to the various command posts. What we saw and heard gave definitely the impression that a massive German effort was under way in a sector extending about 40 kilometers to the south, and 10 kilometers to the west of

Selb, with its rear area reaching into Czechoslovakia. Some of the confusion gave way to more organized preparations for combat action. I saw officers driving around in a couple of small, low-built four-wheel vehicles which I had not seen before; asking about this new type of vehicle I learned that they had been captured from Americans and were called "jeeps."

It was a motley assemblage of all kinds of units and materiel, *Heer, Luftwaffe, Waffen*-SS, *Volkssturm*, Hungarian artillery, and Hitler Youth. I even saw some tanks and armored vehicles. We had never seen such force concentration before. The sight made us crawl out of our apatriotic lethargy which we had become accustomed to. We heard that the *Fuehrer* had ordered Colonel General Ferdinand Schoerner to amass all the remaining German forces for a "decisive" combat action in our area. Later I learned that Schoerner was nicknamed *Heldenklau* (hero snatcher) for his role in scrounging together everybody who could hold a rifle.[20]

Despite this impressive show of force, we boys remained skeptical deep down. After talking to my buddies I told Corporal Liese that we wanted to stay together as a group, rather than being assigned to individual command posts. The hometown camaraderie within our group had become stronger. As the oldest of the boys, I also felt a sense of responsibility for keeping them together, and returning them later to their parents, and Budenheim, fate and war willing (we were not religious enough to bother God with our hope for ultimate survival; we felt he resided somewhere on the abstract level of the "Fatherland," or even above that). Liese finally arranged for us to be kept as a ready pool of messengers and scouts in support of a higher headquarters, regimental or divisional.

For a day or two we were wondering why American combat action was hesitant. This lull seemed to boost local morale somewhat, and rumors had it that this massive show of German force most likely scared the Americans. The first American reaction came in an unexpected form: a heavy raid by hundreds of Allied bombers laid to ruins much of the city of Eger (Cheb in Czech), located about 20 kilometers to the east. Later I learned that it was a major supply hub for our sector. This was the last heavy bombing raid I witnessed, and the only one carried out on Czech soil.

This air raid signaled an intensification of American ground action. American artillery barrages prepared the field for their tanks, followed by highly mobile infantry. German units put up stubborn resistance at places, even launching some local counterattacks. Some points of tactical importance were fiercely fought over. We rushed messages and orders back and forth on our bikes, feet, and bellies, carried ammunition and first-aid material to the front line, and helped evacuate the wounded.

Scouting missions to the hilltops, houses, and trees visually confirmed our skepticism. Where we saw a couple of German tanks, there were 20 or 30 on the other side. Soon German artillery fire ceased altogether, silenced either by American counterbattery fire, strafings, or lack of ammunition. While some German units began to pull back, others were thrown into battle with nothing more than their small arms. Measured by the ideological yardstick of patriotism and demonstration of fighting resolve, some German units may have put up what could be called heroic resistance. It was the courage of desperation in the face of the enemy's overwhelming quantitative superiority. And our population was suffering heavily from this senseless fighting.

How did the locals experience "Schoerner's Last Stand" (and Hitler's, for that matter)? Here are some eyewitness accounts from towns in our sector:[21]

> ...As American troops advanced in eastern Bavaria in April, strafing aircraft fired at everything and everybody that moved on the streets of, and roads, around, Erbendorf. The [Nazi] party appealed daily to the population to maximize defense readiness. Mobile court-martial detachments checked up on the will to defend....Also nonmilitary persons were sentenced to death for weakening the fighting strength, or for lacking resolve to fight, and were executed immediately. A court-martial detachment commanded by a colonel and a major had set up shop in the town hall. After a few days, as combat noise was moving audibly closer, our mayor faked a telephone call according to which American tanks were closing in rapidly; the colonel hastily departed Erbendorf, followed by the major and a prisoner a short while later. The mayor's trick (risky as it was) had worked....
>
> The Americans had, indeed, advanced to the western fringes of our town days before. But now they seemed to have halted

their move. Would Erbendorf be taken by Russian troops, or
the Czechs?...Everybody was horrified at such a prospect....All
public buildings were full of refugees and prisoners of war from
eastern European countries....How would these behave if
Erbendorf fell to the forces from the east or west?...As in all
towns, the *Volkssturm* in Erbendorf received orders to erect tank
obstacles. Thick tree logs were to be lowered vertically deep
into the two shoulders of the road, then logs of the same thick-
ness would be piled up horizontally, between the vertical ones,
to a height of about three meters....For the time being, though,
the logs were just stored alongside the road....

Fleeing his headquarters in Bayreuth to escape the Americans,
Gauleiter (Nazi state governor) Waechter drove through
Erbendorf and noticed that the tank obstacles had not been set
up yet. In his function as *Reichsverteidigungskommissar*[22] ...in
his area of jurisdiction, he ordered the immediate erection of
the obstacles under penalty of the most severe kind. Ironically,
he met with that very fate himself. In the opinion of Hitler,
who had expected him to defend Bayreuth "to the last drop of
blood," he had failed criminally. By order of Bormann,[23]
Waechter was apprehended by SS at the town of Herzogau,
court-martialed, and sentenced to death for cowardice. His
deputy and successor, SS Brigade Leader Ruckdeschel, executed
him on April 19....The tank obstacles were set up....

The *Volkssturm* in Erbendorf consisted of about 30 men who
had been excused from regular military service, or were too old
to serve....We were shown how to load and fire rifles...and to
use the *Panzerfaust*....Two steel plates, each 50 millimeters thick,
were set up as a practice target....Then there was a tremendous
blast, and both plates had a hole in them the size of a large
beet....We *Volkssturm* men received orders to report to an assembly area if we would hear a certain siren signal. Our
commander...told us: "Everybody must come (this was the official part of the order)," and then he added: "But I'd like it
much better if nobody showed up."

In the night of April 18, the local *Volkssturm* commander was
informed that an Army demolition team commanded by a sergeant was getting ready to blow up the bridge across the Naab

River. In order to prevent senseless destruction at the last moment, the local *Volkssturm* commander pretended...that own troops were still approaching from the other side of the Naab and needed to cross the river via the bridge. The pretense worked. The bridge was not blown up, and the Army team pulled out.

A couple of days before the Americans arrived in Erbendorf, a unit of about 300 Hitler Youth...who said they were part of the Mainfranken Tank Close-In Defense Group 34, took positions around our town[24]...but then they requisitioned a tractor with trailer and a team of horses with a wagon, and moved on. The horses and wagon were later returned to their owner....

April 20, 1945, birthday of the founder of the "Thousand Year Reich." We peeked out our attic window and saw the Americans coming....Their infantry approached slowly, seeking cover behind trees. The first tanks rolled across the Naab bridge....A fire fight erupted at the nearby quarry where German Army troops under the command of a lieutenant offered resistance. Several of them, including the lieutenant, got killed....Despite the danger posed by nearby SS units hiding in the woods surrounding the town, an American jeep flying a white flag of truce slowly moved down Braengasse Street....The mayor met them there, and together they disappeared into the town hall. Erbendorf had surrendered....

On Sunday, April 15, Waldsassen was declared an open, unfortified town...and the local *Volkssturm* disbanded. But...the fanatic SS took over the town and surrounding area a few days later and offered resistance which aggravated the situation....On April 17...and April 20...aircraft strafings terrorized the civilian population...of which several were killed...and numerous...were wounded....The morning of April 21 was quiet. Around 12:30 p.m., the advancing Americans began their artillery bombardment of Waldsassen, where some SS still offered resistance....Again, the civilians suffered dead and wounded....The town was ablaze at several places.... In late afternoon, the first American soldiers entered town, which formally surrendered....But in the woods surrounding Waldsassen SS still fiercely fought the Americans for several days....Years later the signs of this battle were still visible...trenches, trees damaged by artillery fire, soldiers' graves....

The wife of a grain mill owner in the area of the town of Mitterteich, approximately 15 kilometers from the Czech border and 10 kilometers from Waldsassen, remembers the last days before the Americans' arrival as follows:[25]

> On April 14, a Saturday, two vehicles with 18 German officers and a field kitchen with cook and driver...requested quarters in the mill....We gave them our living room and covered its floor with a layer of straw....The next morning the highest-ranking officer asked for the time when mass would be held in our church....Some soldiers arrived and asked for their commander. When I told them he was at church, they replied: "We would have loved to go there too"....On April 20, SS dropped in...22 of them. We were scared because we could already hear the Americans fire from the Marktredwitz area. This didn't bother the SS. They were shooting the breeze in our living room, or were standing around in the yard. About 3 p.m. Nazi mayor Protschky sent a man who told us to hang out the white flags....Ludwig showed little regard for the SS and hung out the white flags. Seeing this, a higher-ranking SS got furious. Ludwig advised me to feed them well, and talk to them as little as possible. "They are dangerous," he said. A white flag flew overnight...and apparently the SS didn't take offense any more....Toward evening the firing noise had come real close.
>
> The highest-ranking SS officer asked Resi to take the sewed-on rank insignia off his uniform jacket, which she did....In the evening we were sitting in the large living room together with about 22 undecided SS members. We kept rather silent, until Ludwig...suddenly said to them: "We beg you to leave our mill tonight. The woods are close by; we'll leave the two gates open. Don't you realize the Americans are already at the other end of town?" They didn't say a word. Next morning there were only four of them left in the living room. We thought they were ready to surrender. Ludwig said to them: "You are endangering the many people around here. Why don't you go?" They got up and walked out the door. At this very moment jeeps full of yelling American soldiers came down the street. The four SS members walked up to them, arms raised, and were immediately taken into custody....

On Saturday, April 21, the American soldiers had taken Tirschenreuth. On April 22, their artillery took up positions at Erkersreuth and began pounding the hills between the towns of Rosall and Baernau. Nevertheless...old men, women and children were out to sow the fields. When artillery or aircraft fire hit the fields, they sought cover in sunken lanes, hedgerows, and under bushes....The people here in the village of Ellenfeld adapted to a life on the front line. German soldiers and SS had taken possession of the village, had lost it...and regained it....People with adequate basements in their houses turned them into makeshift survival shelters....The war demanded a high price of the small village. Six civilians were killed...several houses and farms were destroyed...but the ordeal was not over yet. The area between Ellenfeld and Baernau was mined. In a spirit of irresponsible, senseless resistance, the last German troops had placed mines along the way (several farm people were killed by these mines weeks after the war was over).

In March, 1945, the small town of Ploessberg [in the Oberpfaelzer Wald mountains] was made the headquarters of the *Leibstandarde* Adolf Hitler.[26] This was like a nightmare for the non-Nazis in town: This unit exhibited a brisk military activity. A military band concert on Easter weekend made the Nazi-friendly among the population sympathize somewhat with these troops. But as the front-line kept moving closer, the unit relocated, around April 10, to the Bayerischer Wald mountains. Thereafter, retreating *Wehrmacht* units, entirely without command and control, and in mostly deplorable condition, without heavy weapons, and transporting their sparse equipment on self-made hand carts, kept moving through our town.

Volkssturm units, mostly young boys aged 16 from the Rhineland, upset the town with their arrogant behavior. They disregarded the strafing hazard of enemy aircraft...and were shooting at weather vanes and steeple clocks[27]....Thanks to the clever initiative of mayor Wiesender and some bold-hearted men left in town, that group of so-called defenders could be made to leave...before the Americans captured the town. People provided them with motorcycles and bicycles to expedite their departure....Around April 17, there was no more electricity....Public order was collapsing. Spring sowing became risky because of the strafing....In the last week before the Americans took our town, military guards were set up in the streets to get a hold of straying soldiers, and organize them into units for the defense....Combat action in neighboring Schoenficht set parts of that town ablaze....Nevertheless, Catholic mass was held Sunday morning, April 22....French prisoners of war who were quartered in the "Post" hotel came rushing into church to tell the priest that American tanks were approaching. They rolled into town from three different directions....People had to stay inside their houses....White flags were hung out....All small arms and cut-and-thrust weapons were collected and destroyed...and all cameras had to be turned in....

We had a farm in the town of Pleussen....Soldiers were hiding military trucks loaded with spare parts for guns in our barns...to keep them out of sight from strafing aircraft which fired at everything moving on the streets....As the front-line moved closer to our town, we felt more scared....A horrified woman...told us that a young soldier had been court-martialed and executed nearby....A unit of Hungarian soldiers...with horse wagons moved into town. Some local men...asked the commander to have his soldiers take cover inside buildings and keep out of sight of strafing aircraft. The commander became infuriated and pointed his pistol at my father's chest. We were scared to death, but after a while the commander calmed down. In a lull between air strikes, the Hungarians moved on, thank God, to the Gommelsberg Forest....Next, German engineer troops blew up the bridge across the nearby Lausnitz River...as well as big pine trees along the road (to create road blocks)....On April 20, American artillery laid the neighboring town of Konnersreuth in ruins and ashes....That same evening, three young men, 15 or 16 years old, were pushing their bicycles through town. When being asked where they were heading, they replied that they had orders to defend the road between Konnersreuth and Mitterteich. Our neighbor told them to throw their rifles away and stay in his house, the war would certainly be over in a day or two. But they replied that an order is an order, and they were determined to carry it out. They moved on to the location they had indicated....

Around 9 p.m., a *Wehrmacht* officer called my father on the phone and asked whether we could hear small arms fire. After this call the line went dead and remained so until it was repaired several months later....On April 21, we finally saw American convoys move along the road from Konnersreuth to Mitterteich....The three young guys fired at the Americans, and were subsequently killed by American counter-fire....On Sunday, April 22, my father and some neighbors were just having a few glasses of schnapps when the door was thrown open and a submachine gun barrel appeared. A U.S. Army sergeant and some soldiers entered the room and asked whether there were any German soldiers still left in town. We answered in the negative (the last ones had left the night before). The sergeant's second question was whether we had fresh chicken eggs....

A local Catholic priest, who cared for his flock not only from the pulpit, gave this account:[28]

During the last days of combat action, enemy aircraft strafed...the town of Neusorg...its railroad station and the trains more frequently....Tank obstacles were set up at the two entrances to our town. One morning we saw a poster which read: "People of Neusorg! Tear your tank obstacles down, or your town will become a heap of ruins!" As I was suspected of having written the poster, my house was searched by police, but they didn't find any incriminating evidence...nor me. Nevertheless, an SS detachment appeared on April 18, and told the local *Volkssturm* commander—who related all this to me (after I had reappeared from hiding)—that they had orders to hang the Catholic priest. The rope in their hand didn't leave any doubt about the seriousness of their intention. But by radio they received orders to delay the execution until the next day. This didn't materialize, though, because American tanks were already approaching the outskirts of town....

Around midnight, April 19, some bold-hearted men and boys tried to secretly dismantle the tank obstacle at Ebnather Street. But as they were sawing through a tree log, one of the explosive charges hidden inside the obstacle went off, injuring a man, and alerting the party and military headquarters people located in the hotel. This incident caused a tense and dangerous stand-off situation. In the morning of April 20, two of our men took it upon them to approach the Americans with a white flag and inform them about the explosive charges inside the obstacle. Subsequently, the first tanks took a detour and entered Neusorg where the other, smaller tank obstacle had been located. That obstacle was without explosive charges, and had already been removed by the townspeople....Meanwhile, another tank unit was stopped at the obstacle with the charges in it. Suddenly, small arms fire erupted from the woods where SS was still hiding, killing an American officer....The Americans returned fire, and artillery rounds exploded in Neusorg....Our people were finally able to convince the Americans that the Neusorg townspeople did neither have a hand in erecting the tank obstacles nor in the small arms fire....The Americans searched the houses, and moved on....But the danger wasn't over yet. Hiding in the surrounding woods, SS, so-called "Werewolf," kept terrorizing the townspeople for more than a week, breaking into houses at night...until an American follow-on unit finally cleaned out the woods....

Carrying white flags, many soldiers walked from our village of Wendern over to the town of Schwarzenbach to surrender to the Americans there....My father had tears in his eyes, he said who hadn't been through it didn't know how it felt to lose one's freedom....One morning the SS, suspecting treason, set fire to the Holzmueller mill. The owner...was to be executed. Tears streaming from his eyes he asked to be allowed to see his family one more time. His last request was granted, and the next night a soldier escorted him back to his family. But the soldier disappeared in the dark, and the mill owner hid along the stream, thus escaping death....The innkeeper of Hermannsreuth, however, was executed by SS because he refused to give in to them, and remove the white flag from his house. His daughter found his corpse in the nearby woods....On May 1, the Americans took Wendern and immediately opened fire on the towns of Ellenfeld and Hermannsreuth, setting them ablaze. Toward evening an American told us to get out of our house...and we couldn't return until 10 days later, after the Americans had vacated our house....

The foregoing scenes from the final act of a brutally absurd theater are vividly descriptive of the conditions surrounding "Schoerner's Last Stand" in those infamous last days of April 1945. With our good luck holding, my Budenheim group escaped with only two minor injuries, a superficial bullet wound in a buddy's leg, and an artillery fragment's scratch on one of my fingers.

Along with the army headquarters we were assigned to, our group was relocated to a point on Czech soil about halfway between the German town of Tirschenreuth and the Czech town of Tachov. On our way we saw German artillery pieces being blown up by their crews, and ran into a column of about 10 German tanks ("Tiger," if memory serves me right), moving west toward the advancing Americans. They were accompanied by some halftracks, and looked in pretty good shape. Their crews' behavior, and commands, were assertive, and in stark contrast to the general scene of retreat, decay and collapse around us. I walked up to a Panzer soldier and asked him if they were on a counterattack mission. He answered affirmatively, but first they had to secure a refueling point out west. When I told him that the Americans had taken that point days ago, he shrugged his shoulders and curtly replied that those were their orders. There were probably three possibilities to explain the way the Panzers acted as they did. One, they actually were on a counterattack mission which came too late, though, for the collapsing major German effort we were retreating from. Two, they weren't aware of the actual combat situation. Three, they were aware of the actual combat situation and, therefore, decided to choose surrender to the Americans rather than to the Soviet forces rapidly advancing from the east. Number three was the most likely one.

My group had been heading in a south-southeasterly direction a few kilometers from the border for a number of days looking to establish a line. As such, we did not realize we were essentially crossing the American east and northeastward advance at about a right angle. No wonder we were having no luck outrunning them.

This was to become the last major official retrograding action in which our group participated. Apparently our headquarters was trying to set up a new line of resistance (or whatever such embellishing terms may have meant) farther south, and we resumed our messenger and scouting activities in an entirely unreconnoitered area. There were numerous *Waffen*-SS patrolling around the area. To our great dismay they made us turn our bicycles over to them. We reported this to our army headquarters because carrying out our missions on foot would take us much longer. Our feeling toward "our" army headquarters was one of temporary allegiance; after all, they provided us with some rations, and the working relationship between them and us was pretty good. But we dreaded the often arrogant and constantly suspicious *Waffen*-SS. Obviously, the army shared our feeling, and our complaint fell on deaf ears. One of them mumbled something like, "You don't mess around with the SS." Thus, gone were the days of finding out about the latest grapevine news by pedaling to the nearest town, or quickly scavenging the countryside for a bite to eat. Our legs had to get used to being on the run again. Our feet found it harder; dirty foot rags caused infections after the blisters had broken open. To find clean pieces of cloth, and flour to powder our feet, became a major concern of ours. While the chances for saving the Fatherland diminished entirely, our awareness of foot hygiene was on the rise.

Here is a good place for me to present my comments and recollections about the SS, because that subject has been coming up in my memoir. For most of the war I didn't know much about the SS and its Nazi role. Their visibility in my area was generally low until 1944. I don't recall a single SS member among my hometown's population. My father had mentioned some friction between the SA (Brownshirts) and the SS (Blackshirts) in the early 1930s. I also heard that the SS tended to keep a distance from the ordinary Nazi party members. While people had an open chance to size up the ordinary Nazis who lived among them, this was not necessarily so with the SS, at least in the smaller towns.

I remember that one day in 1942 or '43, I was ordered by *Jungvolk* higher-ups to attend a one-day *Jungvolk* leader meeting (I was a *Jungzugfuehrer* then in charge of about 30 boys) in Mainz at which sharp-looking SS officers touted the elitist privilege, honor, and special career possibilities that came with SS membership. Only the best would be selected. Obviously the purpose of this meeting was to recruit volunteers, but I don't know if any *Jungvolk* leaders there volunteered. I certainly didn't.

From Nazi indoctrination I had learned that the SS had been created in the mid-1920s as Hitler's bodyguard, his "political soldiers." Its handpicked members swore absolute faithfulness and obedience to him. During the war the SS was reorganized into the *Waffen*-SS to provide military units for battle. They favored persons from a "Nordic race," blond hair and blue-eyed specimens of a selected elite. This didn't concern me much as I was dark-headed and brown-eyed. I may have met their height requirement for young recruits, but I guess not much more.

After the war, when I read about the SS role, much of the information shed light on the aloofness, arrogance, and a certain veil of secrecy with which they pursued their missions as guardians of the *Fuehrer* and the Reich. I learned that following Germany's initial military successes until 1942, the SS was more successful in winning over the young "Nordic" men in the German-occupied territories, particularly in the Baltic countries, Norway, the Netherlands, Belgium, and Romania, than in Germany proper. Perhaps it was easier for the SS to persuade Germanic-minded young idealists from those countries than from Germany, where the SS could not play the role of liberators. There is no doubt that the SS exploited those naive idealists' ignorance about the inner workings of the Reich. A great many of them had never been to Germany before.

Following the failed assassination attempt on Hitler on July 20, 1944, he and his henchmen lost faith in his generals and the *Wehrmacht* and gave increased responsibility to the SS, his tough, loyal, ideologically reliable and spirited force: the last hope for averting the Reich's total collapse and defeat.[29] Himmler placed SS members in many military, administrative, and civilian offices. In the Reich's closing weeks, I witnessed how the *Waffen*-SS made their public presence felt all of a sudden. By late 1944 we *Jungvolk* boys heard from the grownups about the increasing empowerment of the SS and what people thought about it. These thoughts seemed to spell uncertain fear, which we boys adopted because they came from people we respected. However, the SS couldn't be everywhere in the closing days of the Reich, and wasn't. But I remember them acting as police, checking civilians suspiciously, or in sharp, harsh voices demanding to see the papers of soldiers who obviously were home on leave. We boys at the front had every reason to fear these zealots, and avoided them whenever possible, as did most German soldiers and civilians at that time.

Returning now to the narrative of my retreat into Czechoslovakia, one night as I was on a messenger mission, a shadowy figure lunged at me from behind a tree. I think I glimpsed a knife in his hand, and instinctively pulled my pistol. The figure, perhaps a Czech resistance fighter, darted back into the woods. Should I have fired at him? There it came again, the uneasy question. I would have, had he not bolted, I told myself. I can't remember whether I officially reported the incident. I told my buddies, though, to be extra careful, and to go on nighttime missions in pairs, if possible.

What became immediately noticeable in the airspace over Czech soil was the low enemy strafing activity. Very much to our surprise we saw one day two or three German twin-engine aircraft thunder by at low altitude and very fast speed the likes of which we hadn't seen before. Word spread that these were new Me-262 jet fighters, part of a number of German *Wunderwaffen* (miracle weapons) which General Schoerner still had up his sleeve. But we saw them only once.

The fact that the Messerschmitt Me-262 was the world's first operational jet fighter flown in combat warrants a brief description of its short history. The first model was unveiled in 1939 just prior to the invasion of Poland. Overconfident of an early German victory in Europe, Hitler failed to realize the combat potential of jet aircraft, but the *Luftwaffe* inconspicuously proceeded with its development. When the Allies had gained air superiority over Germany by 1943, Goering's top deputy, Field Marshal Milch, ordered the Me-262's production as a fighter-interceptor. Hitler, however, still obsessed with his ill-fated offensive schemes, wanted the plane converted into a fighter-bomber. When Hitler learned of its appearance as a defensive weapon against Allied bombers over Germany, he called Milch on the carpet. Milch compounded his dilemma by insisting that the aircraft was designed as a fighter and not a bomber. This was too much for Hitler. Despite—or perhaps because of—some signs of increasing insubordination in the *Wehrmacht*'s top ranks, and despite the plane's initial surprising successes in downing a few dozen Allied aircraft, Hitler demoted Milch.

Shortly thereafter, and once it was too late, the *Fuehrer* allowed the Me-262 to enter fighter production. Because of its much faster speed it sporadically scored some successes against Allied bombers and fighters. The U.S. B-17 gun systems could not even track the Me-262. Not fully matured, it had its shortcomings. The two jet engines required frequent overhaul and used much more fuel than the conventional piston engine. Pilot training was inadequate. Overwhelming numbers of Allied fighters patrolled the air space over the few poorly protected bases, forcing dispersal of the jets into individually camouflaged hidings or taking advantage of the terrain.

This brief excursion serves as yet another example of Hitler's idiotic ideas and decision-making. The Allies eventually shot down more than one hundred Me-262s, and the *Luftwaffe* destroyed the ones still intact on the ground before surrendering. So, I am pretty sure the two or three Me-262s I saw whizzing by on a sunny spring day in 1945 over the northern foothills of the Bohemian Forest mountain range were the last of their kind.[30]

Noticeable on the ground were more SS patrols and military police checkpoints. Their main mission seemed to be to catch and collect German stragglers in uniform and civilian clothes, most of them moving in a westerly direction, away from the advancing Soviet front line. Many of them were hastily organized into makeshift units. Schoerner was snatching the last heroes. As there weren't enough small arms around to equip them, we were ordered to turn our pistols over to them. Along with our pistols went a sense of modest security which our paratrooper knives couldn't quite make up for.

We heard that the *Fuehrer* Adolf Hitler was killed in action on April 30 in the battle of Berlin.[31] This news seemed to touch us boys less than it did some adult soldiers who had tears in their eyes; no doubt some were tears of joy. To us boys, Hitler was, or had become, an abstract figure, and the way he was running this war didn't deserve good feelings, anyway. His death just added to our determination to survive this fatherlandish adventure turned Armageddon.

What touched us more, and became of greater immediate concern to us, was the loss of Corporal Liese. I last saw him before a locally limited American attack had separated us. We were unable to find out what happened to him, and talked about him for days, and what a good and understanding leader he had been to us. It is my sincere hope that he survived this insane war.

Our group elected me as their temporary leader until we would find another Corporal Liese. Hans Mueller, a parson's son and my closest buddy, and I secretly discussed possibilities of surrendering to the Americans. But for that purpose, we first had to get out of this *Waffen*-SS-infested area. And in order to be able to do that, we needed an official *Marschbefehl*. That, in turn, could be obtained only if we were again assigned to a regular *Wehrmacht* headquarters or unit. In exceptional cases, a *Marschbefehl* could also be issued by a local post commander, but that approach seemed too risky with all the SS around.

So, on our way southeast, from the Oberpfaelzer Wald into the Boehmerwald mountain range, we kept hugging not only the line of the Czech border, sometimes east, sometimes west of it, but also the finer line of keeping in touch, for a day or two, with an army head-quarters or unit, offering, like temporary hirelings or "soldiers of fortune," our services as scouts and messengers. The tricky part, though, was to avoid getting engaged in direct combat action. In one case, a disgusted headquarters sergeant wrote us a *Marschbefehl* just to get rid of us. God bless him, for this act was to prove a god-send for us.

In another case I remember, it sufficed to identify our group as stragglers who had been separated from their main unit, and had oral orders to catch up with it at some point located in a southeast-erly direction which I picked from my map after making reasonably sure that the new destination wasn't in American hands yet. The drawback of our new modus operandi, though, was that we received food rations only occasionally.

One night I was delivering an order to a small army command post. I had to hand it to the commander personally. After I finally located it, a tired soldier told me I could find the commander in a nearby farmhouse. I got the old farmer out of bed; lighting a candle, he showed me to another room where the commander was in bed, sound asleep. We woke him up, and, still half asleep, he took the envelope, put it on the nightstand without reading it, and wanted to go back to sleep again. But I insisted that he read it, as this was part of my order. He did so in the candlelight and dismissed me. Again following orders, I asked him if he had a return message for me. He gave me a thoroughly disgusted look, answered in the negative and went back to sleep. A day or two later I was summoned to some higher command meeting. At least ten officers were sitting around a large table. One of them asked me whether I had delivered an order the other night to an officer he was pointing at. I recognized him immediately as the one whose sleep I had disturbed. He denied receiving the envelope from me. Beginning to feel uneasy, and in my own defense, I recounted the circumstances under which I had delivered the order. He kept on denying. The officer in charge of the meeting mumbled something like "very well," and I was dismissed. Later, it dawned on me that I might, unknowingly, have been a witness to a court-martial proceeding, perhaps about an officer's failure to follow orders. Although he had put me in a precarious spot by denying what I said, I do hope that officer found enough time to catch up on his sleep when the war was over.

On our southeasterly trek we had reached the Boehmerwald with elevations over one thousand meters. The nights were quite cold, and one morning we saw artillery pounding a mountain slope which was white with frost. A couple of soldiers said that this was the effect of German "icing shells," one of the miracle weapons which would cause the terrain to ice over, making it impassable for American tanks. First we thought they were joking, but they seemed to be serious. Shaking our heads at such wild imagination, we loaded our rucksacks on our transport vehicle, a small four-wheel cart, and kept on pulling and pushing it the roughly 70 kilometers from the Czech town of Domazlice toward Hartmanice.

The sparsity of air strafings over Czech soil and a lull in ground combat made us take things a little easier. We saw fewer SS, though they were still patrolling around the area. But this didn't keep us from taking time to wash up at scenic mountain streams, cut each other's hair, dry foot rags, help out at a first-aid post, and, last-but-not-least, locate a supply point where we might be able to get some food by virtue of our *Marschbefehl*. Civilian refugees from eastern European countries, children and old people, were hanging around for a bite to eat. Some of them had come as far as we had, perhaps 1,500 kilometers or more, but from the opposite direction, running away from the Soviet forces which had advanced to about 50 kilometers to the east of our location. These poor refugees were at an absolute loss for where to go next.

In the assessment of our situation we now had to take a three-fold threat into account: the Americans, the SS, and the Soviets. The Americans posed the least threat in our perception. Finding a good place to surrender to them became now a major concern. Hadn't we heard rumors that the Americans would welcome German POWs with chocolate bars? In long conversations we were trying to adjust our self-respect and pride—or what was left of it—to a new self-perception as future prisoners. I mulled over my conflicting feelings. Sure, the utter hopelessness of our situation, and the total loss of allegiance to the Reich facilitated the thought of surrender. It surely would be easier to do it now. But how would people look at me later, would they call me a coward? Could I look my parents straight in the eye if and when I would return home?

I felt my buddies trusted me completely, with the possible exception of Julius, who had shown ambitions to become the group's new leader, but had been voted down.[32] I felt the weight of making such a decision not only in terms of becoming clear about myself, but also, and more importantly, what was good, and right, for the group; gradually I touched on the subject of a possible surrender to probe the boys' readiness and willingness. They were all in favor. When I tried to get the same response out of Julius, he looked away.

The presence of *Waffen-SS* was less conspicuous on the eastern slopes of the Boehmerwald mountains. With the help of the latest rumors and a map, we searched for a "good" place to call it quits. As we were pushing our baggage cart along a secondary road through the woods, we were suddenly stopped by *Waffen-SS*, their submachine guns pointing at us. As always, I had learned the content of our *Marschbefehl* by heart, and rattled it off to them in accordance with established official routine. They checked it carefully, and then inquired about our weapons. I responded that we had to turn them over previously by *Waffen-SS* order. They eyed us suspiciously and wanted to see a piece of paper attesting to that. The thought flashed through my mind that if there was such a piece of paper, Corporal Liese must have kept it, and I replied as much. After a tense moment they took us around a bend in the road and pointed at a tree from which the corpses of about 10 men were dangling, some of them in civilian clothes. With menacing casualness the SS pointed out to us that we could have ended up "just like those traitors up there," then checked off on our *Marschbefehl*, and let us move on, which we did at no slow pace.

After a couple of kilometers we needed a break to catch our breath in more than one way. Just as we thought the SS had become a diminishing threat, that cruel display of their ridiculous and murderous fanaticism briefly scared us back into the fear and doubt about our idea of surrendering to the Americans (this, of course, was precisely the psychological effect the SS had intended). We felt pretty sick, and I vividly recall our desperate attempts to come to grips with our intention to surrender, and the reality around us.

The sunny days of early May saw us push our baggage cart from the Czech town of Hartmanice southeastward toward Vimperk. There was some artillery activity from the southwest, which meant American, and none from the east at the moment, which meant that the Russians were still a "safe" distance away. We had developed a fine nose for where we could get a bite to eat from the local population. The native Czechs were usually reserved, and hostile in some cases, while the *Sudetendeutsche* (of German descent) were more forthcoming.[33]

As we were winding our way along a secondary road, a fat sergeant of the *Feldgendarmerie* (military police) emerged from a farm house, with a nasty grin on his face, his uniform jacket open over a bulging belly. "Well, boys, let's see what you've got there." He started groping around in the contents of our baggage cart, seemingly looking for some war booty. I showed him our *Marschbefehl* which he just laughed off. When he grabbed a leather jacket I pulled my paratrooper knife, pushed the blade release button and hit his groping fingers hard with the blade's flat surface. I still remember the astounded look on his red face, his mouth open and momentarily speechless. As we pulled away at no slow pace, he shouted something after us that didn't sound very nice. We felt thoroughly disgusted by this guy's behavior. Hadn't we learned early on as *Jungvolk* members that *Kameradendiebstahl* (stealing from comrades) was one of the worst misdeeds?

This incident, in combination with the horrible sight of the dangling corpses, was the last straw in making up my mind about surrendering to the Americans. I told the group as much, and I remember Julius also agreed.

Near Vimperk we found quarters in a friendly farmer's barn. An army supply company was nearby, their trucks loaded with all kinds of edible goodies. With no SS in sight, there just wasn't a better place to await the Americans' arrival. I got in touch with the company commander and joyfully offered our services in view of such a lavish hoard of food. Very much to my disappointment, he declined, but after some gingerly probing of each other's plans it became clear to me that they were ready and willing to surrender as much as we were. I asked him to make sure that not a single shot would be fired at the approaching Americans. He replied affirmatively. My next concern was to get some of his edible goodies. He let go of several sweet high-energy bars which we devoured in no time. Very much to my consternation he made me sign for them as "items issued." I tried to convince him that we needed some more food, and that, from all we heard, the Americans didn't need German army food, but to no avail. In retrospect, his obstinate attitude, and his desire to keep everything under neat control up to the last minute when he would turn control over, even to the Americans, was reflective of a German national character trait fed by Prussian tradition, namely to administrate a public good by bureaucratically correct and rigid rules and in the name of regulations and orders, regardless of the situation at hand. His stinginess brought back memories of the *Luftwaffe* depot at Sonneberg where we had taken common sense into our own hands before the depot was blown up as a result of the same kind of bureaucratically correct, but situationally senseless and idiotic attitude.

Our group was furious, but I was able to calm them down. After all, we also depended for a successful surrender on that company commander's cooperation. Once we were safely in American hands, everything would be different, anyway, and American chocolate bars would probably taste better than that gooey German high-energy stuff.

The next day, May 6, a sunny Sunday, American artillery fired a few rounds into the village without doing much damage. The farmer's family told us to come inside for better cover. After waiting in their living room for about an hour, we heard some sporadic small arms fire, then the intermittent roaring of vehicle engines. I went out into the farm yard to "welcome" the Americans and let them know that everybody was ready to surrender without resistance.

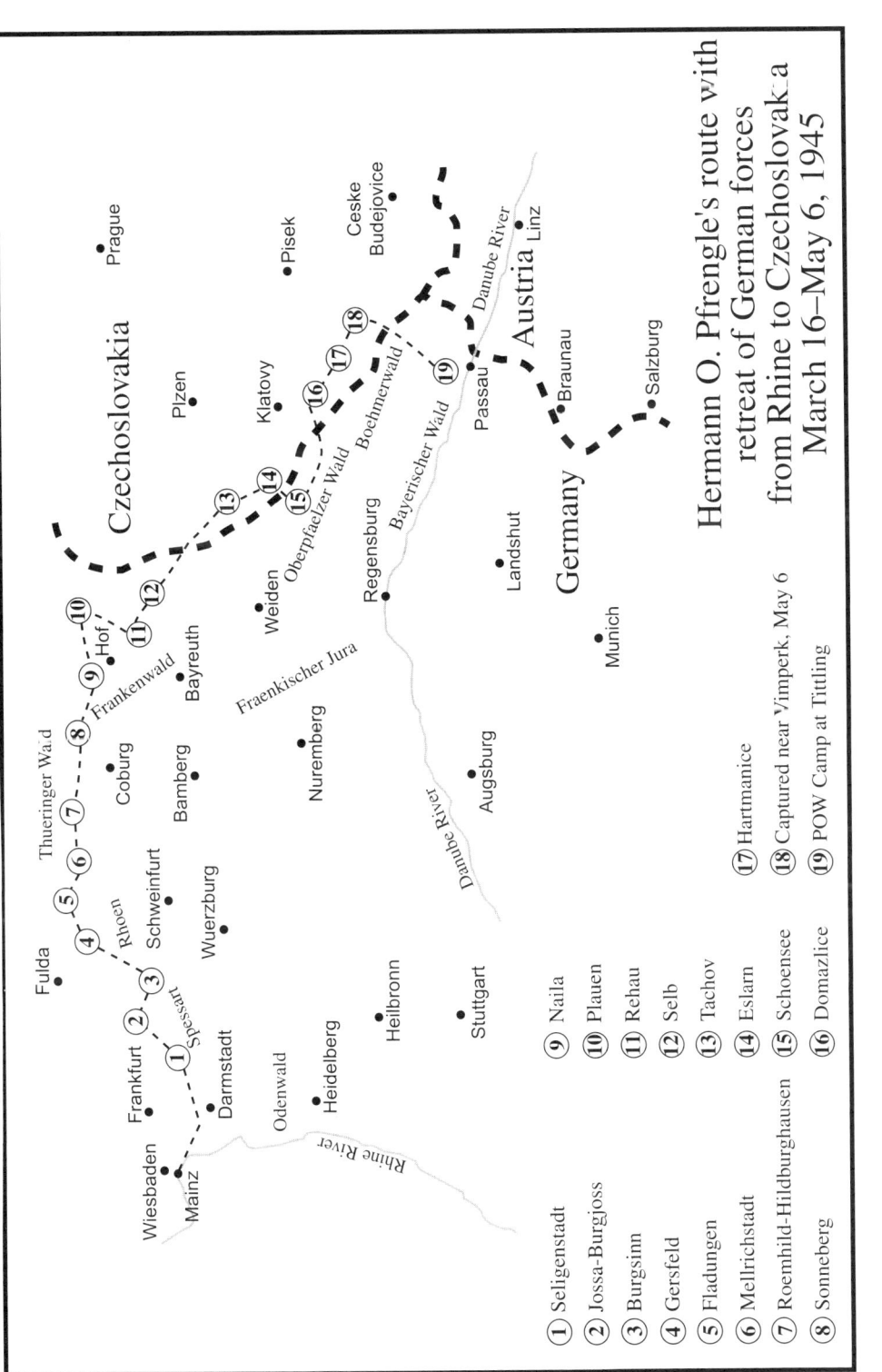

Hermann O. Pfrengle's route with retreat of German forces from Rhine to Czechoslovakia
March 16–May 6, 1945

Czechoslovakia

Germany

Austria

Prague
Pisek
Ceske Budejovice
Linz
Danube River
Plzen
Klatovy
Braunau
Salzburg
Passau
Boehmerwald
Oberpfaelzer Wald
Bayerischer Wald
Weiden
Regensburg
Landshut
Munich
Hof
Frankenwald
Bayreuth
Fraenkischer Jura
Coburg
Bamberg
Nuremberg
Augsburg
Danube River
Thueringer Wald
Schweinfurt
Wuerzburg
Rhoen
Fulda
Heilbronn
Stuttgart
Frankfurt
Spessart
Darmstadt
Odenwald
Heidelberg
Wiesbaden
Mainz
Rhine River

① Seligenstadt
② Jossa-Burgjoss
③ Burgsinn
④ Gersfeld
⑤ Fladungen
⑥ Mellrichstadt
⑦ Roemhild-Hildburghausen
⑧ Sonneberg
⑨ Naila
⑩ Plauen
⑪ Rehau
⑫ Selb
⑬ Tachov
⑭ Eslarn
⑮ Schoensee
⑯ Domazlice
⑰ Hartmanice
⑱ Captured near Vimperk, May 6
⑲ POW Camp at Tittling

Chapter 6

Prisoner of War:
An American Chocolate Bar

Shortly after 4 p.m. on that sunny May 6, 1945, I saw three eyes carefully and suspiciously peeking at me from around the corner of the farm house. Two were human, the third one was the muzzle of an American submachine gun. I stood there, grinning sheepishly, and unable, perhaps out of some stupid pride, to raise my hands. As the first American soldiers rushed into the farm yard seeking positions of cover there, I had the feeling, after a minute or two that they were as relieved as I was at the complete absence of German resistance in the village. Their faces relaxed, some of them smiled or laughed.[1]

They searched me, took my paratrooper knife, but didn't find my personal pocket knife which I had tucked away inside one of my boots. Then I guided them inside the farm house and explained to them in my high-school English that our group was *Volkssturm* and that the farmer's family was as glad as we were to see the Americans. They searched our rucksacks and took my map, personal diary, identification papers, and our *Marschbefehl*. Then we were herded to a nearby POW collection point. Very much to our dismay, we had to leave our rucksacks behind. I asked that we be permitted to take them along, but to no avail. This decision shocked us completely. I quickly retrieved a spoon and hid it inside my pants. One of the German supply trucks had been hit by an artillery round, and the mouth-watering aroma of canned meat wafting from busted cans intensified our hunger pangs. The American chocolate bars we had heard about were nowhere in sight, but the Americans had some of the German food supplies distributed to the POWs. For us it was merely a drop in a bucket. I saw an American try a sticky German high-energy bar, but after a bite or two he contorted his face and threw it away.

At the POW collection point, I found time to study the Americans more closely. They seemed to be out of a different world. Their uniforms and equipment looked so much more practical and comfortable than the Germans'. They moved swiftly in their light rubber-soled boots. I recalled Nazi propaganda in the wake of the 1944 Allied invasion, ridiculing those boots: "The Allies came sneaking ashore on rubber soles." But on rubber soles they won the war. In contrast, the ubiquitous German "short Wellington" or "dice cup," with its stiff, nailed leather soles and worn by the German army since 1870, made for a clumsy and slow gait, and was a torture to the feet. The same unfavorable comparison became apparent as I eyed American small arms. Their carbines, submachine guns, and rifles were relatively light, small and handy, quite a contrast to the unwieldy German K-98 carbine which held six shots of single fire, and whose first model was fielded in 1898—then still the mainstay of the average German infantryman. We were also impressed with the handy individual radio sets that every second or third soldier seemed to carry. With those around, they certainly didn't need messengers. And the multitude of vehicles, combat and others, moving around the area made further comparisons futile. We were simply awestruck by this sheer display of fighting power. How could we Germans ever have thought about winning against such overwhelming quantity and quality of materiel and manpower! No wonder most of the Germans had been kept in the dark about American ground combat power; had we known about it earlier, I'm sure the Germans would have called it quits sooner, I thought to myself.

I also noticed how informally the Americans behaved, and moved about. There was no stiff saluting as a soldier passed a higher rank. Their loud voices had a strange nasal sound to them which made it difficult for me to understand what they were saying, or yelling. Also, many of them seemed to be constantly eating, or chewing on something (months later I became acquainted with the American habit of chewing gum and tried it myself).

After a while, I tried my English on one of our guards, a quiet, middle-aged man, and asked him about his civilian life. He said he was a lawyer, but hastened to add that he was not supposed to speak to POWs. I approached another guard to find out what would happen with us next. He replied that the commander would decide everything, and avoided any further conversation. I was interested in finding out, though, because should the Americans decide to turn us over to the Soviets, who were only about 30 kilometers away, our group would need to make contingency plans for an escape. I didn't dare to tax our guards' patience too much, so I told my buddies that I couldn't get any useful information out of them and, for the time being, to just hang together, rest as much as possible, be on the lookout for food and any kind of cloth, not only for foot rags, but also for protection against the night temperatures which still dipped into the freezing range occasionally. Over there, only a few hundred meters away, was the farm house where we had to leave our rucksacks, messkits, blankets, and extra clothing behind. We were pretty mad at the Americans, and I walked up to a guard to ask for permission to get some of our belongings from the farm house. With a wave of his gun he chased me back to my group.

The hard ground and the cold didn't allow us much sleep, and we welcomed the warming rays of the morning sun like a gift of God. At the moment we weren't so sure, though, that we wanted to include the current circumstances of our longed-for captivity in such divine generosity. We couldn't make a step without being watched suspiciously, or called to order by the guards. Relieving calls of nature became a matter of orders which didn't always coincide with individual needs. I had to suppress the desire to wash up at a nearby stream. What became more difficult to suppress were the constant hunger pangs. There was some distant firing noise from the east, but we couldn't care less. For us, the war certainly was over.

A few hundred POWs, we among them, were loaded on trucks. I tried to find out from our guards about our destination, again to no avail. Would they turn us over to the Soviets? That sinister question hung over our heads like a Damocletian Sword. We stood crammed tight on the truck beds, hanging on to each other to keep our balance. There was no room to sit down. After we had moved over narrow and winding roads for a while, road signs made clear to us that we were headed west. Our faces spelled relief. Rejoicing came to an abrupt end when the truck directly in front of ours turned over in a curve, spilling its human freight all over the road. Everybody wanted to help, but our guards told us to stay put. Leaving behind the accident scene, and its casualties, we continued our trip a few minutes later, at what we thought was a hair-raising speed. The next incident occurred at a steep ascent of the sunken road. A couple of POWs jumped off a truck ahead of us, dashed up the slope and had almost reached its top by the time some guards started to fire and run after them. At the top of the slope they fired some more, then came back. We could only guess the escapees' fate. Off we went again on our breakneck journey to—yeah, whereto? Freedom? That looked so remote. But there was one consolation we shared: at least the Americans didn't turn us over to the Soviets.

After crossing the border into Germany we were unloaded. An American officer told us in fluent German to take our clothes off except for underpants and spread our belongings on the ground. I quickly told my buddies to hide anything personal, such as watches, the best they could, and while sitting on the ground to take off my boots, I tied my wrist watch around my ankle where it was covered by my long johns. With a quick step I made my pocket knife disappear in the ground. The officer told us to turn over anything that could be used as a potential weapon, such as razors, knives, forks, scissors, mirrors, can openers, and the like. If a later inspection revealed that someone was hiding any such item, he would be executed right away. My disappointment in American behavior grew: such rough and tough talk reminded me of some past unpleasant experiences before our capture. It yielded the intended result, though, a heap of "potential weapons."

We passed the subsequent individual inspection without a major incident. All the while I kept one foot over the place where I had rammed my pocket knife into the ground. Thanks to our body odor which had built up powerfully since our last bath about a week ago, the display of our dirty clothes and underwear, and the threat of body lice infestation (which our group was spared because our blood wasn't nourishing enough, I guess), the inspection was not very thorough. At least I heard American soldiers comment disgustedly as much.

The American officer told us what not to do, pointing out the rules which would govern our life from now on, and spiced his words in between with verbal insults. I dimly recall some of his words, such as "lice-infested bastards," his demand to turn war criminals among us over better now than later, and some sneering comparison of our ragged condition with the rubble that was left of the fatherland. At the end of his indoctrination tirade we came to realize that there was nothing left that we were allowed to do, everything was *verboten* (forbidden). In retrospect, I would say this was a partly successful psychological effort to break down our self-esteem, or what was left of it, and with it our will power, thus doing away with any funny ideas about resistance or escape. Total powerlessness and obedience was in store for us from now on. We had been subjected to mind control before, in a different ideological context, though not to such an existentially inexorable degree. I saw some POWs cry. The sight of their tears generated some kind of block in my mind, perhaps a blessing of youth, and I told myself to not let the stuff we'd heard sink in too deep. "Words!" I mumbled to my buddies, and as I pulled my pocket knife out of the ground, I did it with a sensation of sweet triumph, twice as sweet in the face of the humiliation we had just been fed.

The next night we spent in a barn which even had the luxury of some straw in it. Our guards, nice and understanding people, informed us there would be a couple of latrine calls during the night. I acted as interpreter, and we agreed that, following the sound of a whistle, a guard would yell the order "piss!" and those in need would queue up to be taken outside. I will never forget the comical scene of about 30 POWs forming a circle around a manure pit and generating clouds of fog in the cold night air, illuminated by the guards' flashlights like stage lights in a ghostly scene from Richard Wagner's *Goetterdaemmerung*.[2]

When dawn came, I heard some POWs whisper the question for a can opener, a "potential weapon" that had to be turned in the day before. Reluctantly they struck a deal with me: I would open their cans, and would get a can in return. The can opener on my hidden pocket knife did the trick, and my buddies and I enjoyed the delicacy of a spoonful each of salty German meat.

Back on trucks again, we arrived, via the town of Freyung, at the Tittling, Germany, POW camp, located 25 kilometers north of the city of Passau. As we got off the trucks we had to walk a gauntlet of yelling black soldiers some of whom were obviously drunk.

They tried to grab anything shiny or decorative still worn by the POWs, rings, watches, military decorations, rank insignia, and the like. They didn't find any booty on our group, and we just received kicks in the pants. There were some scuffles as POWs tried to resist. It was an unexpectedly crude reception at the camp where we were to spend the next couple of weeks, memorable also because I had never seen a Negro before.

The camp covered a large grassy and soggy depression at the southwestern edge of the town of Tittling. When we arrived it held perhaps a few thousand POWs, but with many hundreds more arriving daily the fences and watch towers were simply moved outward several times during our stay to accommodate as many as about 12,000. There were no buildings or group tents, which meant that the sky was our roof. We were assigned a place from where we were able to watch what was going on around the gate, a welcomed distraction from our daily monotony, slumping morale, hunger, and thirst.

After about two days without food and water we were unable to stand up, or walk, for more than a minute or so, without fainting or collapsing. The worst thing was to see local women with buckets of water at the fence whom the guards kept from passing on the precious stuff to us. There was no appreciable rainfall during the time we were there, and no rain water to catch for drinking purposes. The combination of the bright sun and dehydration made some of us begin to hallucinate. Early in the morning, before it evaporated in the sunshine, we licked the dew from wherever it had collected, including the grass. I wonder what might have gone through the Americans' minds as they saw the Reich's defenders crawling around on the ground like animals.

On a brighter side—if there was one—the mercilessly beautiful weather kept us dry, at least from the top. While the moisture from the soggy ground seeped into our pants, our leather jackets kept us dry above the waistline, and from catching serious colds in the chilly nights. We ate grass which was rapidly disappearing as it was being grazed over by thousands of POWs, and my pocket knife came in handy in digging up weed roots. They tasted as bitter as the fruit of our realization that our captors were punishing us collectively for things we had done, or had not done. If they were intent on breaking our willpower by slowly starving us to death, they were well on their way, we thought. We had reached the level of an animal existence. Corpses were hauled from the camp on an oxcart in the early morning hours. "There comes the hearse," other POWs remarked with gallows humor. We boys avoided the sight of it. Camp life was demoralizing enough the way it was, and we didn't need such a visible reminder of how close death was.

Through the grapevine we heard that an armistice had gone into effect on May 8. We felt absolved, but we were too lethargic to attach much significance to the realization that we had survived the war. We were desperately clinging to the hope for a change in this ordeal, and to somehow survive our captivity. Some grown-up POWs openly wondered why our "liberators" didn't shoot the POWs instead of starving us to a slow death. It would be easier on them and us.

Around the third day in camp we heard that there was water down at the lowest part of the terrain depression, where the camp area had been expanded. We jumped up, staggered a few meters, and collapsed. Other POWs, apparently in better physical shape, kept running toward the source of water. Mustering my last gram of energy I told my buddies to take it easy, and the two youngest ones should go first. They staggered and crawled away. It would have been unwise to leave our camp site unattended; even though it was marked only by torn German army blankets (one blanket per two boys) and some of our clothes we took off during the warm days. Sadly, there were thefts among the POWs. It felt like eternity before the two returned, all muddy in front. Yes, there was a little run. Down on their bellies they had slurped the wet preciousness. When my turn came, I did the same and took in the muddy water in deep gulps. My mind was all greedy body. I crawled away from the run to puke, then returned for more animalistic avidity. I splashed the water in my face, taking its muddy freshness in with every pore—only to get chased away by another POW who was right in shouting at me that the water was for drinking, not washing. Ever since, I have cherished a glass of clear, cool water in a way most people who take it for granted would never understand.

The availability of water let us view the predicament of captivity with more hope of survival. And indeed, things were beginning to look up. We had to form lines of five to receive our daily food rations consisting of a 750-gram can of brothy German beef or pork, brought into camp on *Wehrmacht* trucks operating under American supervision. Divided by five, a 750-gram can made for 150 grams per day, or about three tablespoons per head. Nothing else to go with it. Not enough to live on, but enough to keep a boy from dying. Together with the water and some grass, though, it was enough to reactivate our bowel movements. The latrine consisted of a narrow, open trench whose edges were daily sprayed with chloride powder. It was in full sight of the civilians who lived at the camp's edge. I hope they forgave us this insult to their eyes and noses.

With somewhat revived interest I took in our surroundings. There were not only watchtowers set up around the camp, but also quadruple machine guns mounted on halftracks. To attempt an escape would be suicidal. Beyond, parts of the town looked badly damaged. Our guards didn't care much whether we stayed at our initially assigned camp site, or moved around the camp more freely. They sat around smoking, chewing, conversing, and laughing, and periodically patrolled the camp's fence line. These Americans really enjoyed their role as victors, we thought to ourselves. We also noticed that rank insignia had been removed from most POWs' uniforms. Everybody looked more or less alike, giving the outside appearance of almost total equality, although the ex-officers were easily recognizable by the better cut and material of their uniforms. Some of them still seemed to exercise some authority over their men. During our first days in camp we watched many a German soldier bury his service medals in the ground, only to see them desperately search for their decorations when word spread about a week later that the Americans would trade food or cigarettes for the medals.

Many captors obviously had been less rigorous than ours, because they allowed their POWs to keep their backpacks, most likely with some food in them. We mulled over the unfairness of war in general, and such unequal treatment in particular. Such grousing helped occupy time and mind, but it was not conducive to improving the mood in my group. They began looking to me to somehow miraculously show them a glimpse of light at the uncertain end of this long and dark tunnel. They kept pestering me with their unrealistic hope for some plans. "How do I know?" I responded almost angrily, recalling the popular sarcastic saying as the war was placing ever greater demands on the German soldiers and civilians: "The impossible shall be done instantly, the possible can wait until tomorrow." Their hopes seemed to center around my role as leader, and my English language capability.

Encouraged by my buddies I took heart the next day, walked over to a guard, explained to him that we boys didn't even have backpacks, and asked him about a chance to do some work for food. I was prepared to be turned away, but be it that he had a particularly kind heart that day, or because he just saw the 90 or so pounds of me hanging on to a fence post to stay upright, he said he would see what he could do, and I should report back the same time tomorrow.[3] The mood in our group that night alternated between skepticism and hopeful anticipation.

The next day my buddy Hans and I were there at the appointed time, and so was the guard. Without much ado he told another guard to take us to the nearby German field hospital for "K.P." (U.S. Army slang: "kitchen police"). He obviously overestimated my knowledge of American English, but Hans and I soon found ourselves peeling raw potatoes, mountains of them. We devoured the peels, and a potato, too, occasionally. K.P. was synonymous with paradise. We heard the cries of the wounded in the hospital, which consisted of tents and tarpaulins set up among the walls of a group of destroyed buildings, but the survival instinct made us keep on peeling, and chomping peels. A guard who came after a couple of hours to take us back to camp noticed the bulging pockets of our pants, jackets and overcoats, became suspicious and searched us; I was able to convince him that our buddies back in camp would sure appreciate the extra peels. Our return was a feast for the rest of our group. Sitting close together, they tried to hide their gluttony from the neighboring POWs as best they could. But the best thing was the order to report to the gate again same time the next day.

So I took another buddy with me, and on our way to the hospital the guard, the same one as yesterday, asked me if I could translate a letter to his German girlfriend first thing in the hospital's kitchen. I asked for a couple of sheets of paper, as writing paper always came in handy, and discharged of my complicity in a love affair as best I could. The rest was peeling, thick peels with plenty of potato meat on them. Now and then a guard or a German hospital staff member would come and check on us. I asked if they had some bread or meat leftovers for us, but was told that regulations did not permit that. Some kind soul gave us hot coffee to drink, but it left our bodies the same way it went in. We were happy with plain, clean water. When the guard came to take us back to camp, I asked him for permission to fill some discarded cardboard boxes with potato peels for our buddies. He gave his okay, and we staggered back under our heavy loads, a day's supply for our group.

The next day saw us again happily pulling K.P. which now also included clean-up work around the kitchen. Our lives had found a meaningful content. A German hospital staff orderly told us that the Americans had somewhat relaxed the rules for the treatment of POWs, and things might become easier for us, news which lifted our spirits. Indeed, we were allowed to take flattened cardboard boxes with us that day. They made for good insulation against the moist ground under our bodies. The guard didn't even bother to accompany us all the way back to camp, but rather sent us on our way, remarking something like we ought to know our way by now. My buddy and I took a shortcut through the ruins of some farm buildings where, all of a sudden, we saw a hole in the ground, about two meters square. Its contents made our eyes pop out: knives, daggers, scissors—many hundreds of "potential weapons"! My buddy and I exchanged a quick glance of understanding, looked around, and seeing no American nearby, I jumped into the hole, retrieving about 15 sturdy pocket knives, a pair of scissors and a tiny 2-inch Fin knife, ornamented with a fixed and slightly curved Finnish blade (which I have kept as a special souvenir of my captivity). We hid the "weapons" under the potato peels in our pockets. The whole operation took not much more than a minute.

The significance of the knife was also that it symbolized an act of revolt against conditions that threatened to break us down completely, psychologically and physically. The feeling of doing something forbidden was sweet and satisfying. It preserved a bit of self-respect and represented an action orientation vis-à-vis passivity. The Fin knife helped me to think about the future, some way out of the current demise. As a consequence, perhaps, I mustered the determination and persistence to reformulate my requests for the discharge of our group some time later.

I told the guard at the gate that we had permission to take the flattened cardboard inside. He nodded, and waved us on through the gate. With our pockets bulging with potato peels we must have become a familiar sight to the guards by now, I guess. During the night I was too scared to hand out the "weapons" to my buddies but rather rammed them into the ground underneath my cardboard "mattress." I was pretty nervous that night, but on the other hand it felt good to have accomplished something meaningful on our own, and breaking the monotony and passivity of prison life.[4]

After nightfall the next day, a buddy and I strolled into a section of camp occupied by a few hundred Hungarians, mountain artillery. They had been permitted by the Americans not only to keep their backpacks, but also some food supplies, and pup tents. With all these amenities they clearly were the upper class in our camp society. We approached a couple of them carefully, making sure they were not officers, and told them we had something we wanted to trade for food. Did they have enough food to spare a few cans? That depended on what we had to offer, they replied skeptically. "A pocket knife," I said. After a moment of consternation, their interest gained the upper hand, and following some negotiating we returned with a can of goulash, and two cans of sauerkraut in tomato sauce. Since there was no way to cook it at our camp site, we devoured everything cold, a nocturnal feast under a starlit sky. Unfortunately, the raw sauerkraut didn't agree with our already diarrhetic innards, and the need for frequent trips to the latrine earned me my buddies' annoyance for a couple of days. So they did their own nightly trading visits to the Hungarian section until our arsenal had shrunk to a few knives which we wanted to keep for ourselves as a last resort.

A commotion at the gate woke us from our lethargy one day. About five or six *Waffen*-SS surrounded by shouting American guards were being herded into some kind of sheep corral next to the camp fence. The Americans emptied the SS packs and threw their contents, including packs of cigarettes, cans, and packages of food, into the crowd of POWs who fought over the goodies like a hoard of wild animals. There was not a trace left of the famous, or infamous, German discipline, the spirit of soldierly restraint, or conduct. It had obviously given way to the lowest instincts. The Americans seemingly enjoyed this spectacle, which I found disgusting.

A different kind of spectacle unfolded as a group of Americans approached the fence from outside the camp and guided a couple of men clothed in what looked like striped pajamas into the corral, where they began beating up the SS. Later we learned that these men were probably recently liberated concentration camp inmates. They used their fists and feet to pay some of the misery they had endured under Nazi rule back to the SS tormentors. The guards made sure the SS did not fight back. After some time it looked like they had been beaten unconscious, and the concentration camp inmates walked away. It took us a while to mentally process this brutal spectacle, but we recalled the stragglers hanged by the SS, and after we later learned of the Nazi concentration camp cruelties, we began to understand.

After nightfall that night, we heard some thumping sounds coming from the SS corral, then yelling from the guards. Additional floodlights came on, and there was a lot of commotion around the sheep corral. As far as we could determine, some or all of the SS had escaped. Perhaps they had not been so unconscious after all. Hundreds of American soldiers were combing the area, their flashlights dancing like huge firebugs across the ascending slopes a short distance away. A pile of cardboard boxes was right at the sheep corral, and the thumps could have been caused by the SS men throwing boxes at their guards to distract them. I don't know whether they recaptured the escapees. Next morning, the corral was empty.

Around the time of this incident, the door to our K.P. paradise went shut. No more potato peeling for us. Perhaps other POWs were feasting on the peels now. I remember how some of the other POWs had become suspicious and envious of our K.P. routine, and reproached us for "fraternizing with the enemy." We told them they should feel happy that they were allowed to take some food in their backpacks with them, and to shut up griping. Enraged by our reply, some wanted to start a scuffle with us, but one of their officers, who still seemed to exercise some authority, called them to order and prevented "fratricide over fraternization."

Occasionally, the apathetic mood in the camp gave way to human expressions above the level of animalistic survival. Some POWs formed a choir and sang folk songs, others met for religious reasons, or played cards or chess with a makeshift set. A tall guy so skinny that he could have been hiding behind a telephone pole acted like a preacher, proclaiming that he was a disciple of Jesus Christ one day, and a believer in Hitler the next. Everybody called him a lunatic, but many seemed to enjoy the entertainment. He definitely had rhetorical and theatrical talent, and he broke the camp routine.[5]

After a couple of days he preached his way up to a guard at the gate. Trancelike, his arms stretched out, he slowly approached the gate, neglecting the guard's order to turn back who shouted "in da lager!", using the German word for camp. The guard stepped inside the camp and, knocking him out with a blow to the chin, sent him into a different state of mind. Some POWs dragged him away. This, by the way, was the only time I remember having seen an American inside the camp. We wondered whether the preacher had perhaps put on a fake to get a discharge for reasons of insanity.

Thinking about this incident later, it dawned on me that the guy could be likened to an actor in a theater of the absurd in which even mentally sane people could play the role of disciples of Christ and believers in Hitler at the same time. The Third Reich had set the stage, and Nazi ideology provided the new script for the absurd play. The old, traditional script rooted in a notion of harmony between the idea of the Fatherland and the religious belief system would not have sufficed for Nazi purposes.

Such musings warrant an interlude in recounting my POW camp experiences in order to view briefly the problem of the relationship between church and state in Germany during that time. Of particular interest is why the people did not generally perceive this somewhat unique relationship as a contradiction in terms and concepts, and why in many German homes the crucifix and Hitler's picture were tolerated to coexist.

To be sure, there were exceptions to such coexistence of this-worldy and other-worldly authority. On the local and limited level of my experience as a *Jungvolk* leader, I recall the demonstration described earlier of youthful Catholic dissent in my home town, where I had thought that scheduling our Saturday meetings would accommodate the Catholic boys' confession time. The three boys in question had resolved the conflict arising from the cooperation between church and state by demoting themselves. The church had won out (undoubtedly at the prodding of the priest).

A year later at the prisoner of war camp in Tittling, where I experienced the most severe existential hardship of my young life, among those briefly interned outside the POW camp was a German

Catholic field chaplain, Field General Vicar Werthmann (comparable in worldly rank to a general). In this context, I find it meaningful to contrast his attitude with that of another disciple of Christ, the local Catholic priest, mentioned in the preceding chapter, who demonstrated active responsibility in caring for his flock. In contrast to a needy flock inside the camp, and because he was clergy—and with a general's rank at that—Werthmann's internment was outside the stockade, bringing with it many amenities he apparently took for granted. He described some in detail, including good food in sufficient quantity and relative freedom of movement under American escort. His story, told with traces of indignation and arrogance, showed that conflicts arising from the convergence of church and German militarism against the background of the Nazi regime did not torment him.[6]

But I felt tormented when I read his story after suffering through the POW camp ordeal. How lucky was this high-ranking disciple of Christ? I thought. Nowhere in his diary could I see a stir of care or love for those inside the camp. Not unlike the Americans, he watched the misery from an existentially safe distance outside. How would he have behaved under the duress of the stockade, deprived of the basics of human survival? The tall, skinny, apparently "insane preacher" inside the camp who proclaimed to be a disciple of Christ one day, and a believer in Hitler the next, assumed a new significance in my musings about the absurdities I witnessed and experienced in those days of existential doom. Ultimately, where was the difference between this "crazy preacher" and the field general vicar?

The difference was in the degree of their suffering. Not having personally partaken in this suffering, the field general vicar was able to retain his aloofness over this-worldly matters. From his perspective, I am sure that the traces of indignation and arrogance were not intentional, but merely reflected a feeling of spiritual superiority so firmly rooted in his consciousness that the conflicts which others saw of the converging relationship between church and state, and personified by him, had seemingly become non-issues to him.

From a late-20th-century perspective (particularly the American one), the cause of such issues may have become readily identifiable, shaped as they are by humanistic and enlightened ideas of democracy with its emphasis on more separation rather than approximation

between the two institutions. Werthmann's diary, including his interrogation by intelligence officers, shows how far he had distanced
himself from matters of this world.[7]

> Monday, April 30, 1945...Some young people—intelligence of-
> ficers—occupied themselves with us, especially a chemistry stu-
> dent who had studied in Switzerland and spoke German well.
> Without giving the outright impression of an official interroga-
> tion he starts a conversation whose content centers primarily
> on the mentality of the German people. He is concerned essen-
> tially with the following issues:
>
> 1. How come one can often find the crucifix on the wall in the houses,
>   and at the same time a picture of Hitler?
> 2. The German people share the guilt for so many cruel things which
>   happened in Germany, because the people did not shake off this
>   cruel regime but rather tolerated it.
> 3. The German clergy, too, have brought upon themselves grave guilt,
>   because they didn't fearlessly, and risking their own lives, lash out
>   from the pulpit at, and reject, this regime. Had they done so, ev-
>   erything would have been different, and nobody would have dared
>   to send all the clergy to the concentration camp.
> 4. Why haven't the parents protested against the use of their sons by
>   the *Waffen*-SS?
> 5. The German people display blind obedience and respond to every
>   order with *"Jawohl!"* without considering the moral quality of the
>   order's content....
> 6. Has Hitler officially quit being a member of the Church? Could
>   he receive the last sacraments at the hour of his death?
>
> These are the questions bubbling forth from the American men-
> tality, and finding answers to them is not easy....

I am sure that expecting Chaplain Werthmann to find answers
which might have largely conformed to an interrogator's own moral
value system would have overtaxed the chaplain's intellectual-politi-
cal capabilities. His value system had been shaped by almost two thousand years of religious tradition, with its special church-state
relationship, and all the ups and downs in mankind's secular and religious affairs, rather than by an American viewpoint.

Long before the Nazis came to power, the church in Germany
had come to perceive its societal role as outwardly apolitical in terms

of political activism, but nevertheless made its weight and power felt in dealing with authoritarian regimes and governments, depending on whether, and how well, the purposes and ends of those regimes and governments could be reconciled with those of the church. As such, the 19th-century *Reichskonkordat* (Reich Concordat) became a permanent "peace treaty" between the church and the German state, and has characterized the relationship between the two ever since, including the Third Reich. To appease the churches, Hitler in 1933 had promised to continue the previous Concordat concluded with the Weimar Republic, the government he replaced, and arranged his own *Reichskonkordat* that year with the Vatican.[8]

I believe it was in that light that Chaplain Werthmann viewed the realm of the church, not in humanistic and enlightened terms, but rather in an other-worldly orientation. This becomes explicit in his diary entry of May 1, 1945, describing the first service of the mass the Americans permitted him to hold during his internment:[9]

> I shall not forget this "celebration missae" on May 1, 1945....The guard, equipped with a gun, takes me...to the church...the upper part of which has been damaged by the heavy American artillery bombardment....I celebrate the mass in the catacombs-like basement part....The local priest who, by the way, recognized me as the author of the publication "We want to serve"...acts as my altar assistant. The gray-green figure of the American guard, gun slung over his shoulder, positions himself behind us; he will see, probably without any inner understanding, the unfolding of the "mysterium tremendum."

It also may surprise some that German army belt buckles were adorned with the motto "God With Us." Traditionally, Germans did not run away from God, nor did they use God as a shield. The need and desire to serve a higher authority both in a this-worldly or other-worldly orientation, or the converging of the two as exemplified in the title "Kaiser of God's Grace" only a generation before Hitler came to power, or by the buckles, was a deeply ingrained and societally stabilizing notion in our national character. It should, therefore, not come as a surprise that German history is void of major political revolutions.

After this somewhat philosophical excursion into the politically clear, but spiritually and religiously gray area of convergence of church and state in Germany, let me return to the purely barren earthly situation I was in as a 15-year-old POW of the ungodly war that had just ended for Germany.

The only modern innovation in our camp, as far as I remember, was a public address system. The occasional announcements were mostly depressive or repressive in content, which is why I guess I can't remember any particular one. My mind seemed to filter them out, perhaps a subconscious mechanism of mental self-preservation in order to keep a glimmer of hope alive. We saw what happened when all hope was gone: POWs crying, breaking down mentally, a few of them committing suicide. Outside eyewitness accounts described our camp's situation as follows:[10]

> Many thousands of men...up to 15,000...had to await their discharge under miserable conditions...some of them were turned over to the Russians and saw their home country again only years later—or never....The circumstances in the camp were primitive. Most of the POWs were without shelter, they had to live in the open air. Fortunately, the weather was very warm and dry during the months of May and June, 1945. Sanitary facilities were completely absent....There was only a hastily excavated pit....Food was extremely poor. The daily ration was a can of watery soup from former *Wehrmacht* supplies, and some bread occasionally. Water had to be taken from a small run which flowed through the camp. Charity-minded inhabitants of Tittling slipped food to the POWs although this was strictly forbidden....Wooden shacks were set up which served as a field hospital. Diseases broke out, and POWs died daily; their bodies were hauled away each morning on a cart pulled by oxen. Any remonstration, or lack of compliance with the regulations, resulted in threats to turn POWs over to the Russians located only some kilometers away in Czechoslovakia. Thus, it was easy to maintain strict discipline in the camp....

By the summer of 1945, at least one thing had changed in the treatment of the POWs. The Americans no longer prevented the local civilians from giving water to the POWs, as the following eyewitness account shows:[11]

> The population of Tittling was ordered to haul water to the camp right away to keep the POWs from dying of thirst. My

buddy and I lugged a tub of water from the Willmerdinger fountain, a few hundred meters away, to the camp. The POWs were so thirsty that some of them threw their cans and cups over the fence, begging for water. We lugged the water as fast we could. It wasn't until evening that the situation in the camp had calmed down again....

The sun got hotter from day to day, the run carried visibly less water, the food hadn't improved in quantity or quality, and from the increase of American personnel at the quadruple machine guns as well as along the fence, we could tell that no relaxation of regulations and rules was in sight. Rather, the opposite seemed to be the case, and harsh announcements over the public address system confirmed as much. Perhaps this was a result of the SS escape some days ago. We were looking forward to the cool nights which also made the latrine stench more bearable than during the hot days. Looking up at the stars we would think and talk about a better life, our families, or the past happiness of potato-peeling K.P.

Sometimes we cursed our surrender, and my comrades reproached me as the instigator of the whole thing. Instead, on sometimes regretting our capitulation, we should have gotten hold of civilian clothes and individually found our way back home. In self-defense I raised the specter of getting caught on the way by SS, some Nazi fanatics, or the Americans. At other times, we tried to think up contingency plans in case the Americans would hand us over to the Russians. Fortunately for our sanity, we didn't get very far with this desperate fantasizing; our minds had become too unimaginative. But we were in agreement that it would be better getting shot escaping than dying in a Siberian coal mine.

All the while, in all their reproaching and complaining, my buddies seemed to look to me for coming up with some idea, or that was the way I felt. My frustration grew because I had no idea. Then one of our youngest ones suggested that I should use my English and talk to a guard to arrange for some deal; after all, it had worked with the potato peels. I replied that rules and regulations had been tightened since, the announcements over the public address system threatened stiff penalties for violating rules, and I didn't want to overdo it lest I, or the whole group, end up in a situation even worse than the one we were in right now. Besides, the rules had been tightened so that speaking to guards was strictly *verboten,* too. This meant back to square one, as at the first two days of our captivity.

My buddies' prodding increased my frustration. They had elected me their leader when things were different. I wanted to be left alone now, but couldn't I detect a sardonic smile on Julius' face? When I confronted him directly, and invited his suggestions for ideas, he replied that I was the leader, not he. Paying Julius this form of attention was unnecessary on my part but an act of reaching out to try to bring him in from the fringe of the group. Looking back, the stress and frustrations of this leadership role in these circumstances were sometimes almost overwhelming for a 15 year old, but somehow I kept my wits. Still, I wasn't exactly sure what my responsibilities now really were, but the German officers I watched didn't seem to be so sure about theirs either.[12]

I looked up at the stars, and in retrospect, I don't know why the idea hadn't struck me sooner. Speaking to the guards was *verboten*, but what about writing? I used one of the sheets of paper the guard for whom I had written a love letter gave me, and wrote a petition to the camp commander for our discharge on the grounds that as 13 to 15 year olds, we were not regular members of the *Wehrmacht.* I thought I had used my best high-school English, but when I handed the petition to the guard without a word, he just looked at it, laughed, and tore it apart. When I returned to my friends, I felt like I was running a gauntlet again.

Stubbornness seemed to have become my last resort. I reformulated the request for discharge, using the last piece of paper I had left. The guard's response was as devastating as before. Moreover, some of the neighboring POWs who had seen me walking up to the guard warned me in no uncertain terms not to make any trouble.

My stubbornness turned into desperation. I tried a third time. Out of writing paper, I used a piece of cardboard and again rewrote our petition for discharge. I waited until most of the neighboring POWs were queued up in a food line, then sneaked over to a different guard and handed him our petition, adding only one spoken word: "Please!" He looked at it, folded it up and put it in his pocket. It was a joyous surprise for me, to say the least. Some hope, and much suspense, marked our group's mood for the next day or two.

Around noon, on one of the hot days at the end of May, it took us a short while to trust our ears when the announcement over the public address system was repeated, and we recognized that the names of my group's nine members were being called. The latent fear that we might get handed over to the Russians was swept aside. We had nothing to lose now, and at least might gain a chance to escape once outside the camp, if worse came to worst. Anxiously and cautiously, we reported to the gate as directed, and a guard took us outside to a building where we had to stay near the open door, probably because our POW odor insulted the Americans' noses. Inside, American soldiers were typing, writing, and telephoning in a large office room.

After a while we had to give our personal data: unit designation, home addresses, etc. An American officer asked us some questions, took notes, and I did my best to act as interpreter. Then he gave instructions and some papers to a typist. We stood waiting, peeking outside where freedom was, and would have loved to sit down on the floor, but a sense of growing excitement somehow overcame our physical weakness. I sensed that, with all the waiting and formalities of paperwork, it appeared less likely now that they would hand us over to the Russians. When I remarked as much to my buddies, an American told me to shut up. I gladly obliged. Finally, the officer showed up again and handed each of us a typed sheet of onion skin paper. The top of it read "CERTIFICATE OF DISCHARGE." My eyes popped out, and my buddies could tell from the big grin on my face the good news, before I could open my mouth. I was stammering words of thanks, but the officer cut me short with an impatient gesture of his hand. He instructed us about the general curfew from 6 p.m. to 6 a.m., and dismissed us with the admonition "forget that you have been Hitler soldiers."

I walked outside, certainly much the better for the Americans' noses, trying to grapple with our good fortune and the reality of being on our own. It took us a while to come to terms mentally with what "freedom" meant.[13] Our release was around the end of May, about three weeks after our surrender.

Next we rushed to the nearest public water fountain in Tittling. I don't recall whether we gave the POW camp a last look of farewell, but I'll never forget how we feasted on that water. And the feeling of freedom made it taste twice as sweet. Children and locals congregating around us watched curiously. We must have left them with the impression of strange animals who had escaped from a zoo. Some friendly people brought us a bite to eat, and with their help we turned a shed into a bathhouse.[14]

Gradually, we were again able to strike up a coherent conversation in the group, and though we were tired, we decided to get away from Tittling that afternoon. The town's destruction was more extensive than had been visible from the camp. But mainly we wanted to get away from that camp. At the edge of town we were stopped by an American patrol. We showed them our discharge papers, but they kept us in custody. Our hearts sank. After some radioing back and forth, we got our papers back, and could move on. It took us perhaps two hours to cover a distance of five kilometers, not only on account of our fatigue. Another American patrol checked us again, with the same lengthy procedure, before we were allowed to move on. One of my buddies remarked that the Americans were stricter than the SS. "Yeah, but they don't string people up on trees," responded another one. And what about the American chocolate bar? "Well, maybe later," when our innards would be in better shape for such a delicacy, we consoled ourselves.

Around curfew time we reached a Catholic convent which had been converted to a field hospital, but now it housed only a few patients. Friendly nuns offered us shelter and a supper of bread and smoked bacon. Unfortunately, our stomachs were still used to the culinary level of water and potato peels, and refused these better things that came with freedom. The convent's farmyard fortunately featured some outhouses—with the luxury of paper. We spent the first night of freedom's *Stunde Null* (zero hour, with "day one" just dawning) on a bed of dry, cozy straw, with a roof, not the sky, over our heads, but still God's roof.

In reminiscing about this new beginning, spending "day one" under the roof of a time-honored Catholic institution took on a special meaning in my hitherto Protestant viewpoint of religious matters. Lacking similar institutions, the Protestant Church in Germany did not interface with human misery as directly, proactively, and charitably as the Catholic Church. But I also thought about such difference within the Catholic Church itself. These nuns practiced their religiousness genuinely in good deeds for the needy, and I contrasted this with my previous philosophical musing about General Vicar Werthmann and his other-worldly, theoretical perception of religiosity.

There were about eight of us left from our original Budenheim group, plus Hans Mueller, whose home was Darmstadt. We were all in pretty sad physical condition, suffering from dysentery, somewhat impaired vision, and other ailments caused by malnutrition. Consequently, we didn't make much headway on our trek home. After about 15 kilometers a day on foot, we were exhausted. The luxury of washing up in a farmyard, or a stream, became a drawn-out daily routine. If nothing else, we had time on our hands. We scavenged for food in the villages and towns we passed through. Each of them had public fountains, so drinking water was no longer a problem.

I don't know why the idea hadn't struck me sooner, but wasn't charcoal an old-fashioned remedy for diarrhea? From then on we periodically stopped at burned-out buildings to scratch some charred slivers from the wood. Chewing and swallowing the vile stuff quelled our revolting intestines only briefly. In one village the locals thought we were searching the ruins for remnants of household items, and they tried to chase us away. When I explained to them our actual motive, they stared at us in disbelief. With sarcasm dripping from my black-smeared mouth, I shouted at them: "Not everybody can enjoy the good food you farmer gluttons are eating every day!" My outburst made my buddies and me feel a little better, and we decided not to honor this village with requests for food.

We also began to re-equip ourselves with some basic necessities by means of discarded *Wehrmacht* items we found alongside the road, and soon each of us carried a dented canteen or two, a mess kit, and pieces of tarpaulin in a torn rucksack. Sometimes we would fantasize about the previous owner soldiers, and about their names carved into the aluminum gear. With our spirits gradually revived, we jokingly recalled a Nazi propaganda slogan which said that each single item and piece of equipment counted in the effort toward final victory.

Instead of heading northwest through the Bavarian Forest mountain range—the straightest way home some of my buddies wished to use—I decided to head first southwest to the Danube River valley, a major traffic conduit where it would surely be easier to catch some sort of ride, perhaps even a railroad train. I convinced them that we were in no physical shape to keep on walking through mostly mountains and rural areas. Indeed, as we approached the town of Vilshofen on the Danube, there was more civilian road traffic. Continuing toward the town of Plattling, we enjoyed an occasional ride on a farm wagon, or even a wood-gas operated truck.

Sometimes we would just sit by the roadside for hours and wait for the convenience of a ride rather than expend our energy walking in the hot sun, but all the while scanning the vicinity for something to eat, perhaps only a cherry tree or berry bush. The fruit was, of course, anathema to our diarrhea, but despite all the subsequent running to answer urgent calls, we enjoyed the precious few minutes the fruit stayed with us.

Hopes of catching a train ride did not materialize. Almost all the rail traffic consisted of American military freight trains in the olive-drab color of U.S. Army equipment, and most of the cars were American made. We marveled at the logistical accomplishment of shipping so many rail cars across the Atlantic in such a short time. We mused about the relative logistical advantage of America and Germany sharing an identical railway track gauge, and how German logistics must have been hampered during the Russian campaign by the wider gauge there. "Well, same gauge or not, with all that stuff backing them up, the Americans were bound to win," a buddy stated, impressed as we all were by the huge quantities of supplies moving by both rail and truck, or stacked at frequent supply points.

We had been on the road for more than a week during this early June, but as the impact of our Tittling POW camp memories began to fade, it seemed like much longer. American army patrols checked us a couple of times without much delay and with good nature sent us on our way. Our traveling speed was more and more determined by Hans, who by now unquestionably was the sickest of the group. Moaning with pain, he had to take a rest break about every kilometer. I carried his few belongings, but that didn't help him much. While a sense of ingrained camaraderie prevailed, I heard someone mumble that at this speed we'd never make it home. I was worried. Hans couldn't go on like this any longer. As we slowly approached the city of Straubing, I pondered the best solution both for him and the group. Above all, I was the group's leader through thick and thin, and the boys still identified me in that function. Optimistically I had already pictured the day we would finally arrive in Budenheim together, and my only remaining duty then would be to thank them (though I was unsure if I would find the right words, or whether saying anything at all was appropriate), remind them to see a doctor (as if that, too, was necessary), and plan for a get-together the following week.

On the other hand, while not from Budenheim, Hans had become my closest buddy for reasons mentioned earlier. Back home he had been the leader of a small Protestant Boy Scout group that merged with the *Jungvolk*. Should we leave him behind in the best interest of our group? Sitting next to me at one of our many rest stops, he suddenly said to me, "I know what's been running through your mind. Just get me to a hospital or a place where I can get rid of these damned shits, and take the group on home safely. Don't worry about me. I'll find my way home somehow." His message struck me in the heart.

As we entered Straubing, I had made up my mind. Since we were now free and out of danger, I told my comrades, I would turn over "command" to Julius, who, it must be remembered, had some previous leadership experience, and he would lead them home safely. (About three weeks later, Julius did exactly that.) I would stay behind with Hans until he recovered sufficiently to resume the march home. Julius' eyes flashed triumph with my decision, and he quickly agreed.

My interpretation of personal responsibility certainly must have boosted Julius' self-esteem, but the immediate reaction from the others was mixed. Their desire to get home as soon as possible, however, and perhaps their certain respect for the decision, was enough to convince them it would work. Thanking them for being such a cohesive bunch through thick and thin and for their positive responses to my leadership, I reassured them that my decision was in the best interests of everyone. And please, I ended, let my parents know—assuming they were still alive—why I would be getting home later. "See you soon," we exchanged, and before excessive sentiment took over, we shook hands and parted, Julius and the group heading for the city of Regensburg, and Hans and I into Straubing.

Chapter 7

Padres and Woodcarvers on the Beautiful, Blue Danube: Recovery and Resurgence

Our ears caught the sound of male voices in song in the distance. What a pleasant welcome to Straubing, Hans and I thought. We sat down to rest and listen to their sweet music, "An der schoenen, blauen Donau" ("On the beautiful, blue Danube"), from an operetta by the Viennese waltz king Johann Strauss, and our hearts felt lighter.

As we were rising to leave, two girls, perhaps 17 or 18 years old, approached us and, to our surprise, asked us where we had been. We willingly gave them our story in a nutshell, which they readily accepted. Their invitation to go home with them for a bite to eat, however, flabbergasted us. One was a brunette, the other a blonde, both were pretty, well-dressed, and had an air of class about them. I immediately was aware of our ragged appearance and instinctively wiped my mouth clean of charcoal traces. After a short walk we reached a nice, big, wooden house, where they prepared an eyepopping amount of food. I recall that as our first hot meal in about five weeks. The blonde, a woodcarver, said it was her uncle's house, and the other girl stayed with them.

Looking out the window, we saw a lumberyard with stacks of boards and posts, a few of them disheveled by hits from shells or bombs. Farther away were some sheds and one-level, wooden barrackslike structures. Seeing some outhouses, Hans excused himself hastily, and I was soon to follow. We washed up with the luxury of soap and towels. Shortly the pleasant surprise continued and a man arrived: Uncle Xaver, friendly, middle-aged, who owned the lumberyard and adjoining sawmill. He offered us shelter for the night in one of the barracks. Unaccustomed to such a lengthy streak of luck, we quickly accepted.

Hans needed medical attention, even a hospital, we pointed out, and some time to recover. Uncle Xaver and the girls consulted for a while, and then he walked us to a nearby Catholic monastery which the order of the Merciful Brethren had converted into a make-shift field hospital. We pulled the doorbell chain, and a round-faced, pot-bellied padre appeared, listened to our story, then shook his head sadly in denial. "We are more than full, and can't even provide a minimum of care for many of the wounded." But Uncle Xaver talked him into grudgingly letting us inside to see for ourselves.

The refectory, adjoining rooms, and hallways were filled with cots and double-decker bunks from wall to wall, and each appeared occupied by a patient. The centuries-old high walls echoed with the loud din of human noise, mostly conversations and humorous re-marks yelled across the spaces. My immediate impression was thank God, no serious cases. "Do you want to stay with a crazy bunch of infidels, in a mess like this?" another padre who had taken over for the first asked scornfully. Trusting to our streak of good luck, and sensing this place was as good as any other "hospital" we were likely to find, Hans and I answered together affirmatively. This padre and Uncle Xaver appeared to know each other, briefly exchanging some words in low voices. When the padre heard that only one of us sought admission, he ushered us into a small office and entered Hans' per-sonal data in an oversized ledger. When Hans confessed to being Protestant, the padre muttered something through his beard, and asked, "You are not Prussians, are you?" We truthfully answered no, and he replied, "Good for you!"

We found an empty cot for Hans. When I asked for an oppor-tunity to speak with a doctor or nurse to familiarize them with Hans' condition, the padre burst into roaring laughter. "Do you think this is a spa? We've got a couple of *Wehrmacht* doctors for three hun-dred patients, and we Brethren are the nurses! We've even reduced our normal prayer time—may God forgive us!—just to care for guys like you. Your buddy is either going to make it, or—it's all in God's will." He didn't sound very merciful, nor did Hans look too happy. I comforted Hans the best I could, and told him I'd return tomorrow.

On our way back to the lumberyard, Uncle Xaver told me with a trace of pride that the double-decker bunks had come from his carpenter shop. I thanked him for all of his help and offered to do some handy work if it wasn't heavy work. He took me into the barrack structure where I had two bunks all to myself, complete with straw-filled mattresses and a blanket. "See you tomorrow," he said. What a lucky day, I thought, and later did not remember sleeping as well in many months.

The next morning, the brunette cheerfully surprised me with a piece of bread for breakfast. I ate half and took the other half to Hans. Entering the hospital I found my way to Hans' cot. His emaciated face and sunken eyes managed a smile, but in a weak voice he said he felt lousy, didn't get much food or sleep, and some of his neighboring patients had been rude to him. He moaned, "If you don't get me out of here, I'll die," as I helped him along one of his dashes to the battery of outhouses in the yard.

I went back inside and asked some of his neighbors to be a little nicer and more helpful to my buddy who, while only 15, had nevertheless followed the call to duty as they had. I appealed to these battle-worn warriors' sense of camaraderie. Some looked surprised, others sneered amusingly. "Listen to this snotty brat!" one exclaimed. But then another, with a bandaged arm, said to me somewhat authoritatively: "Don't worry; we'll take care of the baby." Later I learned he was in charge of maintaining some degree of order and discipline among this particular group of 20 or so patients.

I came to realize with relief that this confusion of sick and wounded bodies wasn't quite as disorganized as it first appeared. The food was monotonous, Hans complained, just warm porridge and tea. I urged him to stick with it until his intestines calmed down, and told him I would be back tomorrow with something to read and some more charcoal, though I had no idea whether Uncle Xaver would extend his hospitality.

Back at the lumberyard, the uncle invited me to join him and the girls for a frugal but tasty supper. The brunette saw to it that I got a second helping, and out of the corner of my eyes I began to admire her beautiful long hair and big brown eyes. The uncle's offer brought my mind back to reality: I could stay with them for as long as it took my friend to recover. And in return I would be expected to help with chores and handy work around the yard. I would receive one meal per day. If I wanted more, I would have to scavenge in the nearby villages. I gratefully agreed without hesitation and returned the brunette's glance less bashfully than before. Assured that Hans and I had shelter for the near future, and aware of the hospitality of these good people, I began to feel more confident and safer for the time being, a feeling that boosted my optimism beyond the previous daily uncertainty and restlessness.

The next few days saw me sort out damaged boards, loading some trucks, and cleaning around the sawmill, which because of a diesel fuel shortage was not operating frequently. At first the work was strenuous, but with occasional breaks, regular meals, albeit spartan, and a comfortable bed, I began to feel my strength returning, and correspondingly runs to the outhouse decreased. On a less prosaic level, the brunette's smiles, affectionate words, or just the mere sight of her lifted my spirits.

Each day I visited Hans for an hour or two. He seemed happier to receive some old books and yellowed newspapers the brunette had given me than the bread and charcoal I also brought. He shared the reading material with fellow convalescents, and after a few days I noticed he had begun blending in with their activities, daily group routine, and peculiarities. A doctor had finally seen him and prescribed enemas administered by padre nurses, procedures causing him not only physical discomfort, he confided in me, but also embarrassment. I urged him to endure it and fantasize that a pretty female nurse instead was attending to him. I don't remember whether my rather desperate advice helped, but he got used to the rough treatment. While it made him temporarily weaker than before, his eyes became more expressive, and his words more determined in talking about the future and going home. I sensed he was over the hump and recovering.

A second small bedroom at my end of the barracks was occupied by a woodworker apprentice who came from a village about two bicycle-hours away. Over the weekends he pedaled home and returned Monday mornings with a load of homemade food. After sounding out each other, we became friends. In the evenings he studiously prepared for the theoretical part of his apprenticeship examination. I helped him with some of the mathematics and geometry

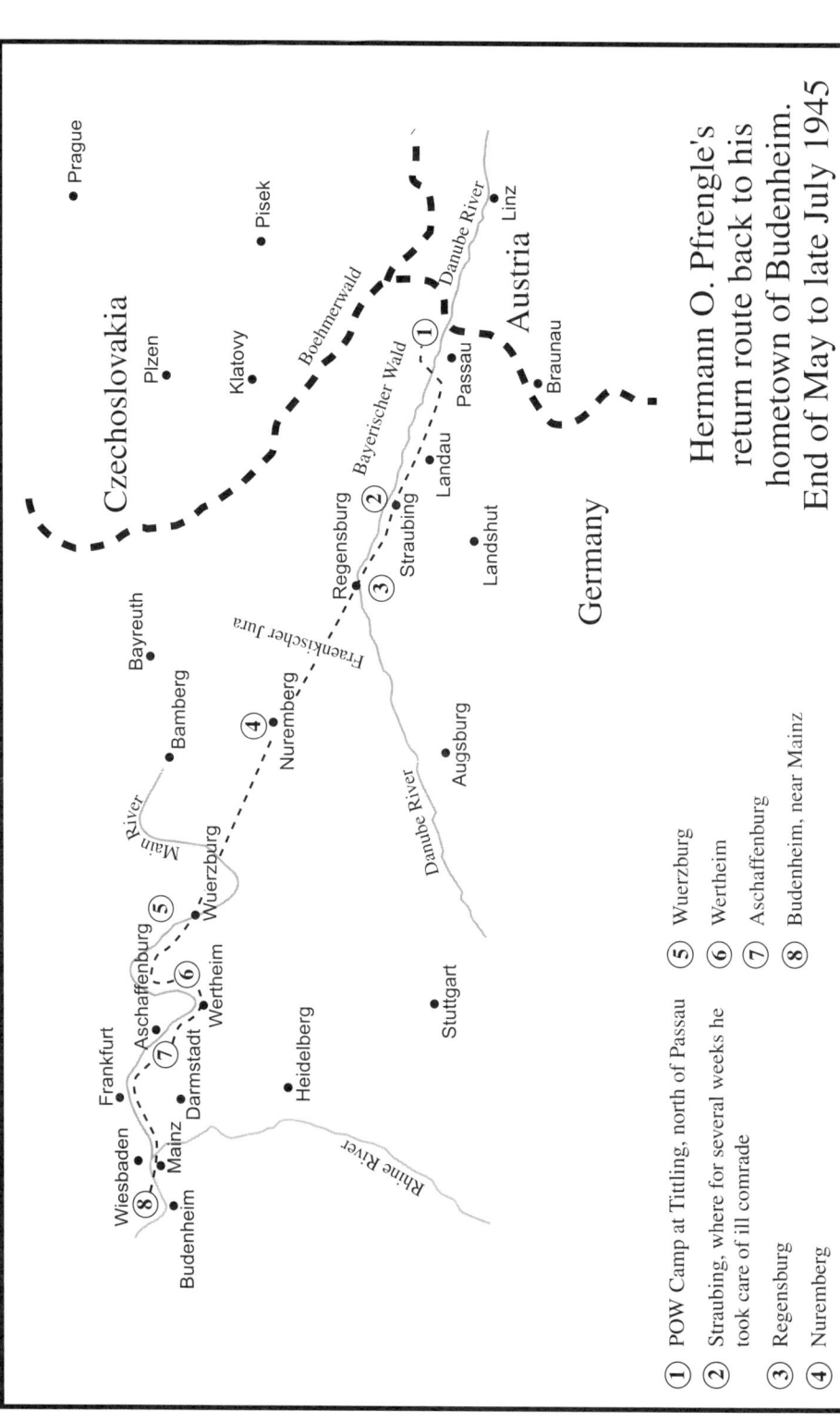

Hermann O. Pfrengle's
return route back to his
hometown of Budenheim.
End of May to late July 1945

① POW Camp at Tittling, north of Passau
② Straubing, where for several weeks he
    took care of ill comrade
③ Regensburg
④ Nuremberg
⑤ Wuerzburg
⑥ Wertheim
⑦ Aschaffenburg
⑧ Budenheim, near Mainz

problems and, in return, enjoyed many a homemade delicacy. Part of it went to Hans who devoured the goodies with mixed consequences, but such indulgence at least lifted his spirits.

The other side of my shelter was occupied by a family of about four who had come from an Eastern European country, probably as forced labor, I was led to believe. But I also heard that some East-Europeans had come to Germany voluntarily, lured by the Nazis' promise of a better life. During the last two years of the war, Xaver's barracks structures had been full of displaced persons (DPs). The males worked as lumberjacks and woodworkers on the premises. By now most of them had left for home or joined the "labor force," a ragtag organization of DPs hastily created by the U.S. Military Government.[1] A few had decided to keep working for Xaver rather than return to homelands occupied by Soviet forces.

One day Xaver's blond niece showed me her woodcarving shop. I marveled at some of the statues and intricately carved pieces of furniture, and casually remarked that I too liked to work with wood, recalling my building of model ships and airplanes back home. "Well, why don't you try it right here?" she encouraged me. Grabbing a block of aged wood, she showed me how to use the various knives and other tools, then left me in the workshop to return later to see what I had accomplished. My mind was more on things utilitarian than artistic, so I began to hollow out a block of wood, gradually shaping it into a square bowl. Using eyeballs rather than measuring tools for dimensioning, I was producing an uneven creation. When she returned, her comment of "pretty good" made me proud—a feeling I had not experienced for a long time. She spoke with her uncle, and the next day my work scene shifted from the lumberyard to the woodcarving shop. How lucky could I get?

The blonde and I became a productive team, turning out furniture legs by means of a hand-operated wood lathe, chair backrests, cupboard door frames, bowls, and other items. She let me keep a few small items with imperfections which I traded for high-quality food, such as eggs and smoked ham, on my foraging trips through neighboring villages. I found time to make a crude chess set which delighted Hans and his fellow patients. An extra effort went into carefully shaping a bowl I intended for my mother. While my partner's presence was emotionally soothing, thoughts of the brunette were more exciting, but also distracting from my ability to concentrate on work.

After suffering a relapse. Hans' health improved visibly, thanks to the unending care by the Merciful Brethren. His intestines began to accept the better-quality food I brought him, and he was able to walk around the hospital. The smelly bedpan under his cot was gone. Sitting in the monastery's courtyard one afternoon, we listened to some of the impromptu presentations of a patients' chorus songs of love, family, and "Heimat," homeland. We hummed along to some familiar tunes and felt the joy of peace and freedom supplant dark memories of war and captivity. Was it only eight weeks before that we were being fired at, only five weeks since we'd thought we'd never survive captivity? It seemed almost unreal. Life was worth living again on this sunny early summer here on the banks of the Danube. We listened to that song again, the lofty "On the beautiful, blue Danube," the one we had heard about three weeks prior upon entering Straubing, unaware that those enticing sounds came from the padres' hospital. What a harmonious atmosphere, I mused, blending proactive Catholic mercifulness with secular joy.

Hans asked me whether I had been able to find out about our families. Not a thing, I replied. There was no mail service yet, and telephones worked locally only, if at all. I had written our home addresses and brief messages on some slips of paper which I handed to people heading in the general direction of Mainz and Darmstadt, along with my request to pass the notes on to others. This was the mode of long-distance communications in Germany in those days.

One day the blonde introduced me to her brother who had just been discharged as a POW. He was in his early twenties, tall, good looking, and self-assertive. In contrast to my POW experience, he had had no bad time in captivity. Soon I noticed that the brunette had a crush on him, and the smiles she had granted me before now went his way. Grudgingly consoling myself with the realization that I could never have been a match for him, and that she was too old for me anyway, I tried to work off some lingering disappointment by putting in extra hours at the woodcarving shop.

On one of my foraging trips, I came across a former German airfield, now deserted, its facilities and few aircraft destroyed. Rummaging through the rubble I found a couple of waterproof aircrew maps printed on yellow plastic, showing the western half of the

Mediterranean and North Africa.[2] Meant for use during Field Marshall Erwin Rommel's campaign three years before, they now came in handy as wrapping material, particularly for a bag of flour which I discovered in a destroyed farmhouse. Some natural protein came with the flour in the form of maggots. Perhaps they would suffocate under the plastic wrap. In any event, this was part of an iron ration which I intended to take along after the good life at Straubing would end. With Hans' health, and mine, steadily improving, we might be on our trek again soon.

From my angle of the world at the fringes of Straubing, there wasn't much of an American military presence anymore, save for some road traffic. But one day a U.S. jeep pulled up at the lumberyard and an officer said he wanted to inspect the premises. Since nobody there spoke any English, I took up my customary role as interpreter. After checking our IDs, the officer wanted to see some papers concerning the premises, which Uncle Xaver readily presented, his hands slightly trembling. Then the officer went on a tour, asking Xaver about the facility, the stacks of wood, its use, and about the workers, an assistant taking notes. He glanced briefly inside the barracks structures, and seeing no one, inquired about their use. Xaver said the workers who had occupied them had gone a while ago. I knew that a few of them were still around, though, and was surprised to see none of them now.

The Americans left after about an hour, and I don't recall whether any of us were able to pinpoint the purpose of the inspection. But I vividly recall the surprised look on the brunette's face as she watched me interpreting, which I pretended not to notice. Letting out a sigh of relief, and announcing that he needed a "Schnaps" now, the uncle filled some shot glasses. Never having tasted the stuff before, and not wanting to upset my intestines now, I declined. The blonde's brother and the brunette toasted each other's health, and he put his arm around her shoulder. That also I pretended not to notice.

With some amusement I saw that the few remaining woodworkers and their families had returned to their usual quarters by nightfall. How, and why, they had avoided the American inspection team, I didn't know, and I wasn't curious about finding out, because everyone appeared to be happy with the status quo.

Hot weather continued throughout the early summer, but the monastery's centuries-old, thick walls provided the patients with some cooling. The mood inside was more relaxed now and the rooms were less crowded; the padre nurses moved about with seeming untiring dedication to their patients. The relationship between both had become jovial. "Heil Hitler, Padre!" I heard a patient jokingly greet his caregiver, who just as so replied that he would have all the incurable Prussians thrown out. Everybody laughed. The sound of a patient's squeezebox enticed some to sing or hum along.

Hans had recovered to where he made the best of his situation and had come to enjoy and share with the activities of others, including playing chess, reading, singing, and even debating questions about Germany, the war, Hitler, and God. "If I don't get out of here soon, the padres might make a Catholic out of me yet," he quipped. I asked the nurse in charge of his group about Hans' condition. "Give our baby another day or two, and he'll be fit to go."

At last, when I came to pick him up, Hans was already waiting in a small office. A friendly padre scribbled something in a thick ledger, and told Hans he was free to leave. We thanked him for the Brethren's care. "Don't thank us, thank God!" he retorted. As a token of our gratitude, I humbly handed the padre a wooden poor box with a carved lid which I had crafted. I said that while we had no money, the box was full of our good thoughts about the Brethren and the monastery. "And about God," he added with a pleasant surprise on his face, before giving us a brief farewell blessing.

About five weeks of partial physical and psychological recovery from the war, a time of existential healing under the humane care spontaneously provided by Uncle Xaver's and God's people, drew to a close. Again I ruminated about the contrast between words and deeds in practicing religion. The Catholic Church, with its active devotion to humanitarian needs, had impressed us two Protestants more profoundly than our own religion had. In retrospect, that experience and a seemingly harmonious blending of art and nature's beauty, coupled with the natives' philosophy of to live and let live, was formative in my lifelong affection for Bavaria.

Following one last cleanup under the makeshift shower I had built between two stacks of wood, we said our thanks to Uncle Xaver and the blonde (I don't remember seeing the other girl that morning). "Why don't you come back and work for me? A lot of rebuilding needs to be done," he said. We all promised to stay in touch once the mails began functioning.[3] The girl stuffed some food in our ruck-sacks, and before the farewell turned too sentimental, we shook hands, and Hans and I set out hopefully on the final leg of our trek home.

Chapter 8

Hobos and Chewing Gum:
The Final Leg Home

Hans and I headed toward the city of Regensburg along the "beautiful, blue Danube," the same route the rest of our group had planned to take five weeks ago. Now in mid-July, we were nine weeks from the end of the war. We made some progress, almost all on foot, with little luck hitching rides, about 20 kilometers a day. We probably could have done better, but I insisted that Hans still take it easy for a while. The awareness of regained physical strength and energy gave us renewed confidence, and occasionally we let our hearts fly by singing.

By the time we reached the city's outskirts, with the help of a piece of map Hans somehow had obtained in the hospital, we located the railroad tracks leading northwest into the city of Nuremberg and followed them for some time, hoping to catch a train ride. Additionally, we figured, railroad tracks shortened the distance between two points more than roads. But walking on the rough gravel bed, forcing our gait into short steps from tie to tie, was very tiring. We welcomed those stretches where a narrow footpath ran alongside the rails. Along those stretches and especially at bridges, we occasionally encountered U.S. guards or patrols. They chased us off the tracks and forced us to continue on a road for a number of kilometers before we could return to the tracks.

We weren't the only civilians choosing the tracks as a route of passage. The entourage included other discharged POWs, refugees, and locals taking the shortest route between towns. One day we approached two Americans sitting on a rail and expected to get diverted. I noticed they were perhaps in their mid-twenties (guessing the age of Americans wasn't easy; compared to the mostly exhaustion-lined and war-weary German faces of the same age, GIs often looked boyishly young and smooth-faced). Bareheaded and wearing pistol holsters, their uniform jackets lying on the ground, their appearance made me guess they weren't actually on duty.

To our surprise, one of them offered us a stick of chewing gum (the first time I tasted some), and then pointed to my wristwatch which I was openly wearing again after hiding it through captivity. In very broken German he asked for the time and gave the watch a closer look. I silently cussed myself for being overly confident by wearing it. He asked me how much I wanted for it, seeming perhaps equally surprised with my reply in English that it was a gift from my godfather, and wasn't for sale. I tried to read his expressions for possible reactions. He could take the watch by force, of course, but not without resistance.

I don't know if he also read as much in my demeanor, but I felt some relief when he started to bargain in terms of "black market currency" with which I was totally unfamiliar. We continued the discourse in English: "Two cartons of cigarettes?" I shook my head no. "Three?" I told him I didn't smoke. He switched his offer to canned food. Upon my persistent refusal, he changed the subject to my English, asking me where I had picked it up. I said it was my five years of German high-school English, and then added weightedly, "I was the assistant U.S. POW camp commander's interpreter" (which had been true on the day of our discharge from Camp Tittling). That probably impressed him, or perhaps he just gave up bartering in view of my naivete at not grasping the value of American cigarettes as a currency exchange rather than a commodity for direct consumption, but he stopped talking about my watch.

To this day I respect his acceptance of my refusal, and besides, the men had not ordered us off the tracks. "Watch or no watch—next time I hope they'll offer us chocolate instead of chewing gum," Hans surmised. Dysentery had intensified some since our Straubing "vacation." I knew about the constipating effect of chocolate and wished we had some then, but not for the price of my watch, which again I hid.

Our food situation improved as barley ripening in the fields was there for the stripping. We chewed the grains for hours. The

Americans had their gum, we had our barley. To break this nutri-tional monotony, I asked a farmer's wife one evening if I could bor-row a pan with grease to make pancakes on her kitchen stove. I broke out the maggot-enriched flour from a place near the airfield, silently hoping she would notice the creatures and offer us something better. She didn't, but added a little milk and salt to the sticky dough. We delved into the crispy end product, Hans not knowing what he was really eating. The next day I counted Hans' dashes, and my runs, behind the bushes. Not knowing whether the ingredients or grease provoked the bowels, or at this point caring, I confidently repeated this nutritional experiment in days ahead.

We were still quite a way from Nuremberg. I don't recall seeing any passenger trains, and the freight trains with mostly German cars came by at relatively slow speeds, but still too fast for us to jump aboard. Sometimes we checked at railroad stations in hopes of snar-ing a ride. While commiserating with our plight, German station operators (who, as traditional government employees, might have served the Kaiser, the Weimar Republic, and Hitler equally consci-entiously) didn't dare disobey their new masters' orders: no unau-thorized riders.

Through the grapevine we heard that farther west rail traffic would increase, and German railroad personnel became more le-nient with hobos. Learning from our railroading experience so far, including our wartime avoidance of air strafings some three months ago by moving at night and staying put during the day, we switched our tactics and hid inside rail yards by the 6:00 p.m. curfew. The logistics drawback, of course, was we cut ourselves off from pos-sible food supplies. But this way we managed to cover the remaining one hundred kilometers to the Nuremberg main freightyard in about two days. On foot it would have taken us about five days.

We were confused over the scope of damage in the Nuremberg main freightyard as we made our way around. It took us a day of hiding in damaged rail cars, and a night of dashing between trains, humps, and wreckage, occasionally bumping into the shadowy fig-ures of other hobos, before a sympathetic railroad worker gave us directions to a train being readied for a trip to Wuerzburg, our next intermediate destination. Carefully unlatching a boxcar door, we sneaked inside and just as carefully slid the door closed. We felt the jolts as cars were being added to the train, but the train didn't pull out. After a few hours, it started to get uncomfortably hot inside the car, despite a small opening in the wall through which we took a stealthful peak now and then, wondering whether we had been overly confident in following the worker's directions.

Our calls of nature had to be taken care of in one of the car's corners. Well into the morning, as we had dozed off, the train finally began to lunge slowly in back-and-forth switching movements. It seemed to take forever before we left Nuremberg behind.[1] Peeking outside we read some station names and, with a huge sigh of relief, saw that we were heading in the right direction. At some places along the way only one of the usual parallel tracks was intact, and we stopped frequently, or switched around, to let another train pass. About halfway between Nuremberg and Wuerzburg, our hunger pangs and aching bones forced a return to our more traditional mode of locomotion, the feet. At dusk we sneaked off the train at one of its stops. The curfew worked in our favor, and we reached a nearby farm without seeing a soul.

We kept walking for a few days, enjoying the luxuries of eating more regularly, and getting enough sleep in a barn or haystack. Singing and waving greetings at the local folks, especially girls (the Straubing brunette had faded to a pleasant memory), we moved at a brisk pace through this lovely northwestern part of Bavaria. But having learned to listen to our bodies, we also took afternoon naps in the shade of trees. I'm not sure if we caught any rides, but what the heck, we felt worry-free and enjoyed peace and freedom each day anew. The thought of our families' uncertain fate, however, the sight of a war-damaged village, a destroyed military vehicle, or a simple cross marking a German soldier's grave quickly compelled a mood change to somber pensiveness, sober reminders that the trauma of war was still with us. We discovered regrettably it would continue to be that way for a long time to come.

Hans and I chatted about the future and rehashed what we might do in later life. The first item, of course, was to finish high school, but after that? Neither of us could be anywhere sure. He seemed not inclined to follow in his father's footsteps and become a Protestant minister. Ironically, my mother had wanted me to become one; she had told me as much when I was a little boy. But later, as I began to display proclivities not conducive to an office of the clergy, she changed her mind, I guess. Now I vaguely mused about doing something in rebuilding Germany, perhaps as an architect or civil engineer. "All this is easier said than done," Hans remarked philosophically. How right he was.

Each kilometer closer to home fed our growing anticipation. We were glad when we reached Wuerzburg but sad when we saw its center, its beautiful baroque churches, completely in ruins. We obtained a little food at a public soup kitchen and decided to try the rails again. Ahead to the west lay the Spessart Mountains (whose western part we had traversed about four months ago in our campaign to save the Fatherland). We figured rails would be faster than trudging our way on hill-and-dale mountain roads, even if we had to wait long hours for a train.

The Wuerzburg freightyard tracks ran along the Main River valley, and we wanted to head down river. At dusk we noticed at least one freight train with its steaming locomotive at the down-river end. The absence of American cars reduced the risk of meeting American guards, and we were lucky. After dark, as the train slowly began to move in the desired direction, we jumped aboard an open semi-boxcar. The train accelerated, boosting our anticipation. If it made it all the way to Aschaffenburg, the next major city down river, we'd be close to home, with only about 30 kilometers left for Hans and about 80 for me.

Our fortune did not hold up all the way to Aschaffenburg. For one thing, we were soaked by heavy rain, the only one I recall in the early summer of 1945. The many tunnels made for brief reprieves from the downpour, but also forced the engine's smoke into our lungs. Shivering, we covered our faces with naturally wet foot rags and cursed the weather. Hans calmed me down with a sentence from the Bible in which he was well versed. Thus, with the help of God and the German railroads, we reached Aschaffenburg by next morning, jumped off, and hid at the foot of an embankment. No guards were in sight, and we walked west.

After finding a bite to eat, as the sun was breaking through, we rested at the edge of some woods and laid out our clothes and belongings to dry. The only dry item in my rucksack was the maggot-enriched flour wrapped in waterproof plastic maps. I opened the bag so Hans could see the flour's protein. Disgustingly he looked at it but gained the upper hand by remarking with his basic good humor, which I had enjoyed so much: "It's a good thing you won't find another chance to feed me that stuff again; but the Bible says God lives in even the smallest of beings." "Amen," I added.

Taking it easy, we spent most of the day drying in the sun, dozing, and discussing what might lie ahead on arrival home. We promised to keep in touch.[2] He set out to thank me for successfully leading our group through thick and thin, and for staying behind to help him during his hospitalization in Straubing. I wasn't used to such encomium, and humbly replied that I had merely done what I had learned and felt about responsibility and camaraderie. "You'd have done the same thing," I responded. But deep down I was pleased to hear it from my closest friend of the group.

We finished a last supper together in a farmhouse and parted early the next morning. Hans headed southwest toward his hometown near the city of Darmstadt, and I walked west-northwest toward Frankfurt. "Mission accomplished," I said to myself. Well, almost, for there was one final obstacle. How would I get across the Rhine? My last attempt at that task, as I was reconnoitering a way home in mid-March, had been in vain, as the German army had blown up all the bridges. Now I heard rumors about the Rhine being some kind of check line to be crossed only with a special pass which would be difficult to obtain.

I spent the night south of Frankfurt, procured some food the next morning, filled my battered canteen with water, and headed toward the large freightyard between Frankfurt and Offenbach. It was rather busy, and to my consternation I saw other hobos climb on or off the trains in broad daylight. The nearby German railway workers appeared not to mind. I relaxed a bit and watched the scene from behind a cover. When I saw hobos and workers talking freely with each other, I took heart, walked up to a couple of them, and asked about getting across the Rhine to Mainz. "Sure, the Americans have built an emergency bridge with one track across the river," a worker answered. Then he casually added that I should take cover again because an American patrol would come through at a certain time on a routine check of the freight yard.

I hid in a damaged car, and the other hobos disappeared too. I marveled at how well this informal information network functioned.

When the patrol came by I watched them from my hideaway as they walked along the tracks chewing gum and laughing, stopping here and there to talk to a worker, or read some cargo manifest attached to the loaded cars. Once the patrol had gone, the hobos reappeared. I left my hideaway, and with the help of the information network soon found myself aboard another semi-boxcar slowly moving toward the Rhine that early evening. The car crawled at walking speed while crossing the one-track trestle just south of Mainz built on top of the demolished railroad bridge that had spanned the river. The trestle creaked and squeaked and shook under the train's load. It seemed like hours before the whole train was across. As we gained speed on the other side, a load as heavy as the train's came off my mind.

Shortly the train stopped at the Mainz freight yard. Nightfall was setting in, and it was well past curfew time. I was particularly careful in making sure I could sneak off the train undetected, but as I squeezed my way between two damaged cars, an American voice yelled, and I froze. Despair flashed through my mind: was my long journey about to end just 10 kilometers from home? I readied myself for harsh words, to say the least, but the American only quietly checked my POW discharge paper and asked me a few general questions. Hearing my English, he became almost friendly, and waved the beam of his flashlight in the direction of rows of damaged passenger cars, instructing me to remain inside one overnight until the end of curfew at 6:00 a.m. "Don't leave the car before, or you will be in trouble."

I spent the night on a hard wooden bench. The stench of human feces, much worse than Camp Tittling's latrine aroma, kept me from falling asleep. But with the warning in mind, and my hometown only a two-hour walk away, I wished to take no risk by changing cars. I forced myself to look at the bright side: I was 10 kilometers from my house, would sleep in a bed the next night, and the guard hadn't taken me into custody, although he certainly knew I had arrived by probably illegal means.

The next morning found me briskly heading toward my hometown of Budenheim, winged by anticipation, leaving the outskirts of the heavily damaged, partly destroyed city of Mainz behind. A surge of joy filled my heart at seeing the familiar sight of my town's houses. Walking past the railroad station, I noticed some war damage to the building, but when I turned on to my street, I saw with tremendous relief that all houses were intact. My mother and I rejoiced in having each other again, and I tenderly cradled my 15-week-old brother, Roland, in my arms. My father had not returned yet from his forced adventure to save the Third Reich, but we had word that he was alive and well. It was late July 1945. I had been gone more than four months.

With war behind, people everywhere coped with the challenges of a new beginning. Quickly mine was cut out. I worked as a farmhand to feed the three of us. Survival continued to remain the only substantive objective, for much longer than I had thought would be the case. But peace, and freedom from the Nazi burden, gave it an entirely different meaning.

Hermann Pfrengle with his brother, Roland, 1949

Adoptive father, Dr. Otto Pfrengle; brother, Roland; Hermann Pfrengle; mother, Luise, 1949

Epilogue
Doing the "Right Thing"

Including the Straubing interlude, my trip home had taken about eight weeks, part of it on foot, ample time to recover some from the physical and psychological hardships imposed as the price of freedom. I returned in late July 1945, more than four months after departing for the front.

En route home, the joy of having survived, and the ability to move about with relatively few restrictions had made life worth living again. Romantic patriotic dreams, and the boy-scoutish adventurism of saving the Fatherland, had given way to a temporarily blissful blank on the surface of my mind. Without the burden of material possessions, and rid of the ideological ballast of Nazism, its perverted ideals and war machine, I felt existentially happy during those summer days of June–July 1945. Living from day to day, I felt like I had been reborn.[1]

With the memories of POW hardships withdrawing to the back of my mind, watching American soldiers in a more peaceful, everyday environment brought forth feelings of reassurance and friendliness. While I had yet to taste my first American chocolate bar, many a German child came to enjoy the Americans' generosities. And was it not thanks to one American guard's individual initiative, who went beyond his duty as a soldier, that our group was discharged early? I mulled over the issue of orders and obedience, and how difficult it can be to do the "right thing"—not to blindly follow orders. That American guard lives on in my memory as an example of

146

how even a strict order can be carried out humanely. The only other such example that comes to my mind in reminiscing about the war's last couple of months is Corporal Liese. Both men of the rank and file, in two opposing armies, deserve my and my buddies' thanks more than words in this book can express.

On my way home I saw a poster signed by General Dwight D. Eisenhower informing the German public that courts to be set up by the military government would determine the degree and extent to which the German people were responsible for the war and the atrocities committed by the Nazis. Gradually, and in a fragmentary fashion, I learned about the concentration camps and the inhuman cruelties committed there. All this was so horribly shocking that at first it sounded unbelievable. The poster's message didn't directly touch me very much at the time, as I thought that none of the folks I knew were capable of committing such atrocities. But I also thought of the German men who had been hanged by the SS in a tree. If they could do this to Germans, what were they capable of doing to people of other nationalities, races, and ethnicities? I asked myself later, as the problem of a people's collective guilt kept stirring in my mind. In writing my memoir, the following item crossed my desk:[2]

> The fact that people could be so cruel on such a large scale means that there must be something evil...few ever admit to being victimizers....There are lots of things that you don't want to do but are forced to go along with....I watched others being beaten too many times to count. I felt bad, because I was older and thought I should do something. But I didn't. As you watch more and more, you get jaded....I was very eager to join...otherwise I would feel disgraced....

Such might have been some of the soul-searching, self-critical remembrances of an erstwhile young Nazi hothead who had been induced, and ordered, to do certain things in the name of the party's ideology pretending to serve the people's and country's best interests, things of cruelty and brutality by humane standards—except that the above quotation is from remembrances of participants in Mao's Chinese Communist revolution. In a historic comparison, it helps to show that authoritarian regimes and their radical ideologies can have the same dehumanizing and devastating effects on the minds and actions of naive believers the world over.

What also emerged in later retrospect was the question why, at Casablanca in 1943, the Allies made German unconditional surrender the only way to end this war. The English military historian Lidell Hart called it "the most expensive and consequential formula of history."[3] As debated by historians since, I also asked myself, what if the German military would have been given the chance of conditional surrender, instead of having to keep on fighting, true to their oath of western tradition, to their total defeat? At the least, it would have driven a decisive wedge between the German military and the Nazi regime. At the most, the German military might have been encouraged to desert the already visibly doomed cause of the Reich and "its war," thus bringing about the regime's collapse.[4] Could millions of lives have been saved that way? Would it have been the "right thing" to do? These were among the questions I pondered later as I was trying to find explanations for the purpose and conduct of this war, and my own tiny involvement in it.

Even from a purely military perspective, the continuation of the fighting was utterly senseless once Germany's natural western defense line along the Rhine had fallen (which, in the face of the overwhelming Allied fighting power superiority, was more symbolic than strategic). In addition, the *Wehrmacht*'s fighting spirit and morale had been broken some time earlier. In this war, the Germans were geared to and thus great in the offense, but were inadequate defenders, as that was counter to Hitler's thought processes. Fighting continued because there was nobody willing or capable of putting an end to it as long as the man responsible for the war was still around. A week after he had removed himself, the war was over. But the final report issued on May 9, 1945, by the Supreme *Wehrmacht* Command *(OKW)* still sounds more like a self-righteous eulogy than a realistic, responsible, and honest assessment of the immediate situation Germany (the Fatherland)—not only its military, but its people as well—found itself in, as the following excerpt denotes:[5]

> ...The *Wehrmacht* has ceased the hopeless fighting. This brings to an end almost six years of an honorable struggle. It has brought us great victories, but also severe defeats. In the end, the German *Wehrmacht* has succumbed honorably to an immensely superior force. The German soldier's accomplishments, performed in the best manner for his people true to his oath,

will remain forever unforgettable. Under severe sacrifices the home front has supported him with all its best efforts. The unique performance on the front line and the home front will find its ultimate appreciation in history's later judgment.

The German soldiers' accomplishments at sea, on land and in the air will not go without the foe's respect. Standing tall, every soldier can, therefore, put his weapons down with pride and, in this gravest hour of our history, put himself to work for our people's eternal life.

In this grave hour, the *Wehrmacht* commemorates its comrades killed in action. The dead commit us to unconditional faithfulness, obedience and discipline toward the Fatherland which is bleeding from countless wounds.

This had the hollow ring of ill-fated patriotism, but there was not a word of criticism, or even accusation or condemnation, about the political regime whose orders the *Wehrmacht* had, more or less willingly, carried out. In such a mental vacuum, fostered by a pathological, self-serving separation of military from political business, there ran no room for perception of conscious evil perpetrated by the Reich's political and most of its military's leaders. In an eye-opening way I came to recall high-school memories of Machiavelli's teachings, who spoke admiringly of men who cared more for their homeland than for the salvation of their souls, and who adhered to the tenet that patriotic ends justify the means.

But for the time being, what I felt in those post-war months, above all, was the joy of survival, gratitude, and the certainty: "Never another war again!"

H. Pfrengle, *right*, on assignment to the U.S. Military Assistance Advisory Group in Bonn, West Germany, inspects U.S. tanks and equipment received by 5th German Armored Division, 1958.

H. Pfrengle, *second from left*, with the U.S. Military Assistance Advisory Group on maneuvers with first III Corps exercise in West Germany, ca. 1959

The Pfrengles, Hermann and Otto, in Wiesbaden home, 1960

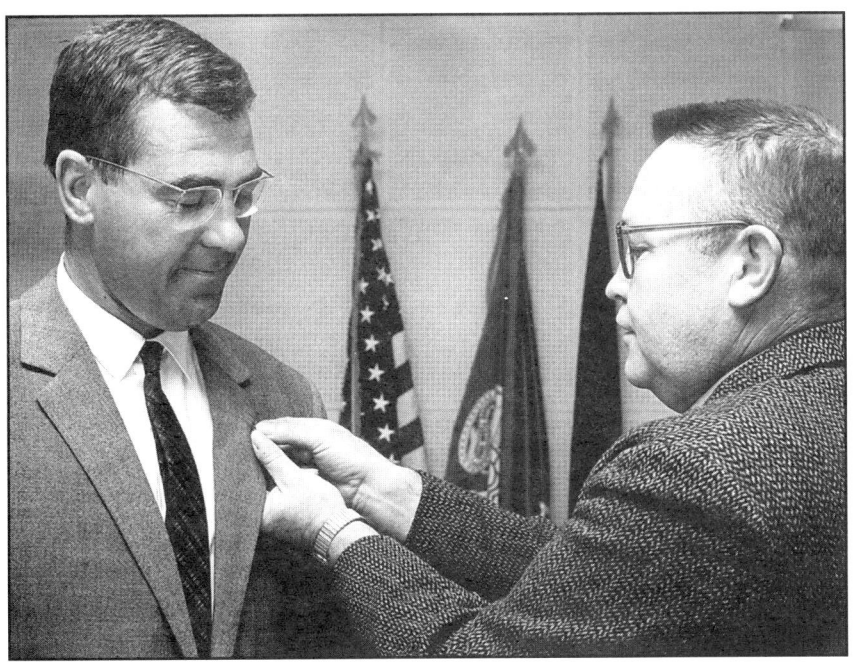

H. Pfrengle receives U.S. Civil Service award, U.S. Embassy, Bonn, West Germany, in 1963.

H. Pfrengle with his German boss, Rolf Rodenhauser, Aberdeen Proving Ground, Maryland, 1970

H. Pfrengle at his Arlington, Virginia, office, 1979

153

H. Pfrengle lecturing on multinational program management, Department of
Defense Systems Management College, 1980

H. Pfrengle addresses International Economics Symposium, University of
Erlangen, West Germany, 1982. *Seated,* Professor Oswald Hahn, chairman

About the Author

Hermann O. Pfrengle

After a break of almost two years, Hermann O. Pfrengle continued his high-school/junior-college education in Geinhausen, graduating in September 1949. From 1950 to 1953, he studied architecture at the Technical Universities of Darmstadt and Stuttgart. But the bachelor's degree in architecture (equivalent) no longer served his personal or professional aspirations. The dawning of the Cold War made him realize that safeguarding survival, peace, and new-found freedom in a democratic Germany necessitated more than building aesthetically designed houses.

Becoming convinced that post-World War II reconstruction could thrive only in a firm Western security framework, his redefined professional aspirations turned his educational interests to international relations and cooperation. Along these lines he worked his way through university courses geared to his new goal, and, in his enthusiasm for many things American, prepared himself for "working with Americans." Interestingly, about 40 years later this became a major topic of his lectures at the U.S. Department of Defense Systems Management College (DSMC), of the Defense Acquisition University, Fort Belvoir, Virginia.

In 1955–56, H. Pfrengle worked for U.S. Consulates in Germany under the U.S. Refugee Relief Act. He then entered the diplomatic arena at the American Embassy in Bonn. After completing a technical course program and graduating from the Munich Language School, he was promoted to assistant research and development

154

(R&D) coordinator, U.S. Military Assistance Advisory Group (MAAG). Here he finally received his "American chocolate bar," referred to in his memoir, albeit in a form very different from what he envisioned as an American prisoner of war. His American reeducation effort had come full circle.

To help initiate closer cooperation between the two countries in industrial and defense standardization and specifications, the Federal Republic of Germany (FRG) Office of Standardization appointed Pfrengle to its Terminology Committee. Involvement in the MBT 70 Program, the first major U.S.-FRG cooperative R&D effort, gave him the opportunity to work in the United States. In 1966, he was transferred to Detroit, Michigan, along with the U.S.-FRG Joint Engineering Agency. In 1969, he became an FRG liaison officer at the Headquarters, U.S. Army Test and Evaluation Command, Aberdeen, Maryland. Beginning in 1972 he was assigned in the Washington, D.C., area, and was instrumental in establishing and operating R&D liaison activities with the Department of Defense.

In the late 1970s, his duties expanded to include cooperation within the North Atlantic Treaty Organization (NATO), and Canada was added to his office's area of direct responsibility. His work also involved contacts with the U.S. Congress and Departments of State, Energy, and Commerce, and other agencies. He also served as interpreter for heads of state, including in 1990–91 international meetings for President George Bush and German Chancellor Helmut Kohl.

Being a lifelong learner, H. Pfrengle earned a BA degree from Oakland-Michigan State University, and an MA and MLA from The Johns Hopkins University in sociology, international politics-international economics, and completed course work for a doctorate in international relations at The American University. At DSMC, since 1978 he has been a guest lecturer, and since 1988 an honorary international professor. He has written numerous articles and several contributions to books, and delivered many presentations and lectures on NATO, international defense acquisition management, economics, and related topics. In recognition for his work, which focused on the cooperation between the United States, Germany, and other European countries, he received several awards from the U.S. and FRG governments.

Some of his latest writings, ranging from economics, politics and management to literary issues, have been published in American magazines and newspapers. Other retirement activities include volunteer work for a local amputee support group, a homeowners' association, and an occasional game of chess. His marriage to Iris M. Wiersdorff ended in divorce. Their daughter, Claudia, lives in Germany. Now residing in Herndon, Virginia, he remains active in the international arena.

Hermann Pfrengle, ca. 1959, with U.S. Army Liaison Officer LTC Paul Kinneson, *left,* and a U.S. Air Force liaison officer, *right,* at a German NATO Liaison Center

Hermann Pfrengle in front of the White House, Christmas 1994

About the Coauthor

Wilbur D. Jones, Jr.

Wilbur D. Jones, Jr., a University of North Carolina history graduate, is an author and military historian in Wilmington, North Carolina. A retired navy captain, he has written numerous books and articles on military history and national defense issues, specializing in World War II, the Civil War, and weapons acquisition. He speaks and lectures widely on those topics, including at UNC-Wilmington.

His most recent books are *Hawaii Goes to War: The Aftermath of Pearl Harbor* (WWII - White Mane), written with his wife, Carroll Robbins Jones; *Condemned to Live: A Panzer Artilleryman s Five-Front War* (WWII - White Mane); *Gyrene: The World War II United States Marine* (WWII - White Mane); *Giants in the Cornfield: The 27th Indiana Infantry* (Civil War - White Mane); and *Arming the Eagle: A History of U.S. Weapons Acquisition Since 1775* (Department of Defense Systems Management College Press and Government Printing Office).

He served in political staff positions in the Nixon and Ford administrations, including as assistant and advance representative to President Ford, served as an assistant to two cabinet secretaries, and assistant to two California Members of Congress. In 1996 he retired after nearly 41 consecutive years of service to the Department of Defense, the last 12 as a professor at the Defense Systems Management College, Fort Belvoir, Virginia. He also is a retired professional baseball and basketball official at the NCAA Division I, high school, and recreation levels.

A Wilmington native, he moved back home in 1997. He served as volunteer chairman of the three-award-winning Wartime Wilmington Commemoration, 1999, a year-long series of activities paying tribute to the area's boomtown role in the World War II war effort, and the men and women who served in uniform and on the home front. He has recently written a book, his 14th, on the history of the Wilmington area during World War II, tentatively titled "A Sentimental Journey: Memoirs of a Wartime Boomtown," and is leading a campaign to establish a World War II home front museum in Wilmington.

His current civic activities include service as vice president, Friends of the Battleship North Carolina Memorial; member of the New Hanover County Library Advisory Board; director of the Wilmington Council of the Navy League; and director of the Wilmington Rotary Club.

He has been married 42 years to Carroll, of Los Angeles. They have three children: Patricia Jacobson, of Michigan; David, of Raleigh, North Carolina; and Andrew, of Wilmington. They have raised their only grandchild, Carrie, since she was two. She is a senior in high school in Wilmington.

Notes

PREFACE

1. Franz A. P. Frisch and Wilbur D. Jones, Jr., *Condemned to Live: A Panzer Artilleryman s Five-Front War* (Shippensburg, Pa.: White Mane, 2000.)

INTRODUCTION

1. H. Pfrengle addresses the "miracle of Dunkirk" later in this book.

2. The German *Westwall* was a continuous series of tactically connected reinforced concrete pillboxes and emplacements extending from Basel on the Swiss border north to Kleve on the Dutch border. H. Pfrengle and his *Jungvolk* unit helped build parts of it. Principal weapons in the primary line consisted of 37mm antitank and machine guns, with some limited artillery in open earthworks, and field fortifications for infantry. The concrete installations in general were 20–30'x40–50' horizontally, and 20–25' high, of which about half was underground. Walls and roofs were 4-8' thick and sometimes steel-plated. The secondary line was a lighter and intermittent line of defense. "Where a natural attack corridor existed (...the Moselle River valley...) there the defenses were most dense....The object of the defenses was not to stop the enemy but to slow him up and to tire him in the attack and then hit him with strong counterattacks." [*First United States Army: Report of Operations, 1 August 1944–22 February 1945*, 51-52.]

3. I. C. B. Dear and M. R. D. Foot, eds., *The Oxford Companion to World War II* (New York: Oxford University Press, 1995), 469.

4. This command authority, established in August 1944 after Hitler distrusted the army, was characteristic of his desperate attempt to squeeze the last potential for defense from the people. *Volkssturm* members Pfrengle talked with after the war stated they had never seen a single SS man involved in *Volkssturm* activities.

5. H. W. Koch, *The Hitler Youth: Origins and Development 1922–1945* (New York: Barnes & Noble Books, 1996), 112.

6. Ibid., dust jacket.

7. The *Reichsarbeitdienst* provided cheap labor for many public works projects including the Autobahn. Subsequently men were usually drafted into the *Wehrmacht*. One of Pfrengle's best hometown friends went through this process and never became, or was coerced to become, a Nazi party member.

8. Hans-Christian Brandenburg, *Die Geschichte der Hitlerjugend* [The History of the Hitler Youth], Second Edition (Cologne: Berend von Nottbeck, 1982), 11 [translation H. Pfrengle's].

9. Koch, 272; and Brandenburg, 169.

10. The large majority of these *Jungvolk* leaders were secondary school students. Their exemption from membership in the Hitler Youth organization was legally based on Nazi decrees concerning youth movements. The objective was to build and maintain a leadership corps exclusively for the *Jungvolk* units. Dr. Alfred Schwinger, an expert on German constitutional law of the 20th century and international law, provided this information. For more on the above distinction between the *Jungvolk* and the Hitler Youth, see Jurgen Herbst, *Requiem For A German Past: A Boyhood Among the Nazis* (Madison: University of Wisconsin Press, 1999), 37–63. Both sources also share H. Pfrengle's experience that the *Jungvolk* had only loose ties to the Hitler Youth. The fact that both sources had been *Jungvolk* leaders adds to their qualifications as primary sources.

11. Artur Axmann quoted in Koch, 248.

12. Koch, 250.

CHAPTER 1

1. The regular work week for employees at my father's place of business was about 44 hours, with Sundays and Wednesday and Saturday afternoons off.

2. The approximate educational equivalent of a combination of American high school and junior college, with academic emphasis on natural science, mathematics, and three mandatory foreign languages..

3. *Jungvolk* (young people) was the second class (for 10–14 year olds) of the *Hitlerjugend* (Hitler Youth), a senior organization for 15–18-year-old boys and girls. Membership was compulsory in both. For the distinction between the two, see this book's introduction.

CHAPTER 2

1. Less than two years later, Germans sarcastically referred to Goering as "Herr Meier."

2. *Wehrmachtsberichte*, or "Armed Forces Reports," were brief, daily, selective, and favorable media summaries of combat action for public consumption.

3. "Gold Pheasant" was a nickname for the brownish-golden uniforms of higher-up, full-time Nazi officials, as distinct from the somewhat "lowly" Brownshirts.

4. When the war began, selected per capita rations were as follows (per week):

   23 oz. of meat
   21 oz. of dairy products
   4 oz. of marmalade or 2 oz. sugar, oil or lard
   5 oz. of grain, cereal or tapioca

   By the end of 1939, the weekly rations were approaching austere quantities, as carbohydrates increasingly took the place of proteins:

3 oz. of butter	4 oz. of marmalade
3 oz. of margarine	8 oz. of sugar
2 oz. of lard or bacon	4 oz. of grain or cereal
2 oz. of cheese	1 oz. of tapioca
5 lbs. of bread	3 oz. of *Ersatzkaffee*
1 lb. of meat	

   [Sources: *Arbeitsgruppe Lokalgeschichte*, Oleg Cernavin, *Budenheim im Dritten Reich*, Budenheim, 1985; and *Mainzer* Journal, August 25, and December 20, 1939]

5. At least 43 soldiers from Budenheim lost their lives in the war, and more remained missing in action.

6. As I learned later, these courses also were designed to pre-select potential officer candidate "material," something neither my parents nor I were aware of at the time.

7. In retrospect, I am sure that they, along with the owners of the *Rittergut*, were part of the Protestant Church's "inner resistance circle." One of the most prominent displays of dissent against the Nazis came from a former *Jungvolk Faehnleinfuehrer*, Hans Scholl, who with sister Sophie led *Die Weisse Rose* (White Rose), a Protestant youth resistance group in 1942

originating in the city of Ulm. In 1943 the Nazis beheaded both Scholls, once enthusiastic members of the Hitler Youth.

8. When they came in the summer of 1944, the *Flak* batteries had been moved to some other locations.

9. German teachers and university professors have been state employees ever since the late 1800s. The basic idea was that, as employees with lifelong job security, they would stay aloof from the vagaries of any given political regime, and, in concentrating on academia, provide for a continuously high level of education. But this idealistic educational concept has been violated more often than not, in that they became servants of the political ideology in vogue at any given time.

10. As its name implies, the Gestapo's activities were usually secretive and directed toward the "underground." The Gestapo had about 35,000 informants in a population of 80 million citizens (see Peter Schneider, "Invisible Man," in *Los Angeles Times* Book Review, 22 June 1997, 8).

11. As I learned after the war, the perfumery owner had made secret provisions for his survival by stocking a cave in an abandoned quarry with canned food and other survival implements. The tinware factory's co-owner was allowed to keep his own private automobile throughout the war—an unusual privilege at the time. In 1945, he met the approaching U.S. troops in his car, flying a white flag, and negotiated a peaceful surrender. Subsequently, the U.S. Military Government instituted him as the new mayor of Budenheim.

12. The bombing of cities took on a discernible pattern. First to come were the pathfinders, setting smoke and lighted signals—which we called Christmas trees—to mark the target area. Next came the intermittent waves of block busters and incendiary drops, sometimes followed by more precise signal marking of point targets. A certain type of block buster bombs generated a pressure wave which not only made sturdy buildings collapse, but also human lungs. Some soldiers on home leave commented that this was worse than front-line fighting.

CHAPTER 3

1. When I revisited the area 34 years later, most of the pillboxes and bunkers had been demolished, a few of them by Allied action. But some behemoths had withstood the demolition charges, and were now used as barns or as storage sheds for construction material. Some had even been converted to weekend "cottages," with decks and small wooden structures added on; what a peaceful, almost idyllic, contrast to see flower boxes in firing ports!

2. The American-built *Mustangs* were particularly feared by the Germans because of their low-altitude capability, high firepower, and low engine noise level.

3. The German word for battle is *Schlacht*, the verb being *schlachten*, which means "to slaughter," and what I saw around me was a slaughter field.

4. An abbreviation I guess every G.I. is familiar with: "same old shit."

CHAPTER 4

1. Later my father would remark that, with officers like that, we couldn't win the war, but they made the best out of losing it.

2. By late 1944, railroad travel in Germany was more difficult to obtain as the Allies repeatedly bombed and strafed tracks, locomotives, and cars. No longer did the trains run on time (or as often). This reminds me of the Nazi slogan: *Raeder muessen rollen fuer den Sieg!* (Railroad wheels must keep on turning for the victory!).

3. An early German form of radar.

4. In the 1940 lull (the "Phoney War") between the invasions of Poland and France, British soldiers sang a musical boast, "We're Gonna Hang Out the Washing on the Siegfried Line," anticipating the quick collapse of Germany's *Westwall* once attacked.

5. All the bridges across the Rhine and Main Rivers in our area were in constant use at the time, and I often wondered why the Allies, who must have known of those conspicuous German troop movements from east to west, didn't knock out these bridges as systematically and

methodologically as they were bombing the big cities. Granted, low cloud covers often prevented point target attacks, and Allied aircraft dropped water mines into the upriver portions of the Rhine and Main, but they did little damage in striking an occasional bridge pile. Most of the mines were rendered ineffective by means of deflectors and traps, or were demolished in our area by the *Flusspioniere* (river engineers with boats) stationed at the Schierstein harbor near Wiesbaden. In retrospect, I suppose the Allies wanted the bridges kept intact for their own crossings.

6. Nazi propaganda lingo in 1944 referred increasingly to the "people," and de-emphasized use of the notions of *Vaterland* and Reich, which apparently had become too abstract for propaganda purposes in the face of the war's realities. Ironically, that year Nazi ideology seemed to undergo a shift in its proclamations toward more recognition of the "people." This desperate "democratization" approach was, of course, the Nazis' last ideological resort after the notion of the *Vaterland* was deemed less appealing as its most visible manifestation, the military, was being defeated, and the Reich, with its political and social institutions, was collapsing. Reportedly, shortly before his suicide on April 30, 1945, Hitler cursed most bitterly the German people. It was they who had deserted him, and for that they deserved total defeat.

7. Food hoarding and black marketeering were declared crimes early on in the war, but many committed them anyway. Farmers were difficult to control and check. Some got caught. It came to be tolerated later, depending on the degree of Nazi spirit prevailing in a community's administration. Needless to say that many little and big Nazis benefited personally from such "illegal" activities as well.

8. For a new and detailed narration of the Ardennes offensive by a Panzer officer, see Helmut Ritgen, *Westfront 1944 Remembered: From Normandy to the Ardennes* (Winnipeg: J. J. Fedorowicz Publishing, 1995).

9. Later I learned that all available aircraft capable of taking to the air, including nonmilitary and sports planes, had been mobilized for this last-ditch effort.

10. In Hamburg and Kiel a "Swing Clique" and "Swing Youth" were identified which listened and danced to "decadent" Western music from foreign radio stations. This was a dual violation of Nazi regulations. The Gestapo report on this matter speaks of the need to counteract with all severity such attempts to undermine decency and morals, and the fighting morale of the German youth, and in the worst cases, recommends placement in youth detention camps. [Hans-Christian Brandenburg, *Die Geschichte der Hitlerjugend* (The History of the Hitler Youth), Second Edition (Koeln: Berend von Nottbeck, 1982), 212]

CHAPTER 5

1. The matter of whether authority existed to "draft" us *Jungvolk* into active service perhaps is aptly answered in this story of a *Jungvolk* unit's last days of combat in 1945 near Berlin: "Our leaders...and the police fetched us from our homes....My *Jungzugfuehrer* who refused was strung up on the nearest tree by a few SS men and an SA man. But then he was already fifteen years old...." [H. W. Koch, *The Hitler Youth* (New York: Barnes & Noble Books, 1996), 250] Concerning the *Flakhelfer* role for which I was to be drafted initially, the authoritative order said: "The boys shall be assigned only duties which correspond with their age." [Brandenburg, 231]

There was method behind this highly ambiguous wording. While the boys were ordered to perform soldiers' duties, they were considered legally as mere military "helpers, assistants, or support personnel." These two examples clearly show how unscrupulously the Nazis treated "legalities" as a basis for forcing minors into combat service, a violation of the Geneva Convention. The Nazis didn't give a damn; all and any means were justified to achieve the *Endsieg.*

2. We didn't know at the time that the American Ninth Army on March 7 discovered that the Remagen bridge, about one hundred kilometers northwest of us, though damaged, was usable. It promptly forced a crossing and established the first Allied bridgehead across the Rhine, which on March 25 became a spearhead for attacking into the heart of Germany. I think I crossed the Rhine west-to-east on a bridge from Mainz to Kastel.

3. Either there was no German artillery in this area, or it lacked ammunition; most likely, both assumptions were true.

4. Strange as it may seem, we were heading west for home, unlike almost all other Germans on the move who were headed east. Budenheim was on the west bank of the Rhine. The territory we wanted to cross into was probably occupied by advance parties of Americans, including even the western outskirts of Mainz. The distance between us and the enemy was between 2–5 kilometers across the Rhine. If that were the case, surely he must be spending the night in our Budenheim.

5. Later I learned that the Americans—elements of General George S. Patton's Third Army—had indeed crossed the Rhine at Oppenheim-Nierstein on March 22, about 20 kilometers south of Mainz and a few kilometers south of Trebur, and were advancing northeasterly toward us.

6. Ria Fischer (administrator of the Babenhausen city archives) to H. Pfrengle, March 5, 1996.

7. Literally "*Flak* helpers" were boys who performed anti-aircraft gun crew functions except those of the gunner's who was a regular soldier.

8. *Marschbefehl* were marching, or moving, orders showing, among other things, the intended destination or movement of a unit or person.

9. Guenter Sagan, "*Die Zerstoerung von Hauswurz 1945* (The Destruction of Hauswurz in 1945)," in *Fuldaer Zeitung*, February 21, 1996 (translation H. Pfrengle's).

10. MGFA No. B-360, Munzel, Oskar, Generalmajor *Panzerausbildungsverband Thueringen* (Tank Training Combat Command Thuringia), (U.S. 2nd Armored Division), 27 March to 5 April 1945. General Munzel wrote his report, parts of which have been excerpted above, in February 1947 in the U.S. POW Camp Allendorf (translation H. Pfrengle's).

11. General Munzel did not mention the fact that we boys, as messengers, scouts, etc., played the mobile role in these liaison activities. But, perhaps, he didn't even know about our existence there, just as he was in the dark about many other things pertaining to his sector's defense; communications were that poor.

12. On that day, my group was in ready position in Flieden, which I remember precisely because of the holiday sequence Good Friday to Easter Monday.

13. Meaning the "tank-destroyer" tanks. These were of a casemate design, i.e., without a rotating turret, which made for a lower silhouette, lower weight, and higher speed. Their specific purpose was to kill tanks.

14. Organizationally, *Flak* was part of the *Luftwaffe,* not the *Heer.* Until this uniform makeover, our group had worn the standard *Jungvolk* uniform of dark blue jackets, trousers, and caps.

15. This was a typical "latrine rumor." In reality, by no genius we had merely moved temporarily away from the main thrust of the American attack.

16. Adolf Hossfeld, "*Der Zusammenbruch im April 1945 in Sonneberg* (The Collapse in April 1945 in Sonneberg)," in *Neue Presse*, January 30, 1993 (translation H. Pfrengle's).

17. Herbert Schneider, in Hossfeld.

18. Helmut Hoehn, in Hossfeld.

19. Manfred Bock, in Hossfeld.

20. As a historical note, Schoerner, commander of Army Group Center, was promoted to field marshal as the unfortunate recipient of Hitler's final major decree to the *Wehrmacht*, a totally impossible task which never could get underway.

21. The following series of eyewitness accounts is taken from: *Volkshochschule des Landkreises Tirschenreuth, Arbeitskreis Heimatforschung,* in *Bittere Zeiten* (Bitter Times) (Pressath: Eckhard Bodner Publishers, 1995) (translation H. Pfrengle's).

22. *Reich* Defense Commissioner, the highest Nazi authority for matters of defense in his area of jurisdiction; his role, and actions, often conflicted with those of the *Wehrmacht.*

23. After the failed attempt on Hitler's life on July 20, 1944, by army Colonel Claus von Stauffenberg, Martin Bormann became a sort of Nazi chief of staff for Hitler.

24. In my recollection, they were assigned front-line coverage right next to our unit.

25. *Bittere Zeiten.*

26. Hitler's own SS Guard Regiment, reputedly the most crack and elite of all German units.

27. Most likely this group was from our unit. They talked about shooting their automatic rifles at strafing aircraft, and the church steeples got in the line of fire, or so the story went.

28. *Bittere Zeiten.*

29. The first visible reaction we civilians noticed after the attempt on Hitler was that the old, traditional way of military saluting was changed to the way the Nazis saluted each other, with the right arm stretched out. Hitler ordered it for everybody, but I remember the sight of many a front-line hardened soldier who would keep saluting the old way and then, with a sly grin and faking embarrassment, abruptly stick his arm out and mumble something like, "excuse me."

30. "That it did not make a bigger impact was not due to any airframe shortcomings, but to engine problems, interference from government departments and, in the later stages, from Hitler himself....There is no doubt that if the type had not been held back through engine and political problems it could well have tipped the scales in Germany's favor by breaking up the Allied day bombing program." [David Mondey, *Axis Aircraft of World War II* (London: Chancellor Press, 1996), 186, 188]

31. Weeks later I learned that he had cowardly taken the easy way out by committing suicide. I felt contempt for him.

32. Back home in Budenheim, Julius had become *Jungvolk* leader No. 2 by a "buddy-buddy" relationship with the No. 1 leader. Shortly the boys began to dislike Julius, and No. 1 replaced him with me. I guess Julius never forgot it, perhaps harboring some "professional jealousy."

33. The *Sudetendeutsche* were expelled later. Their property was confiscated by the Czech authorities, still an issue in the political relations between Germany and the Czech Republic as late as 1996.

CHAPTER 6

1. From the best I can determine now, the likely unit we surrendered to was an armored division (4th probably, or 90th Infanty Division) from Major General S. Leroy Irwin's XII Corps of Patton's Third Army. The U.S. Army's official history cites XII Corps' advance in this area: "...the drive into Czechoslovakia was at first an anticlimax. The fighting was unreal, a comic opera war carried on by men who wanted to surrender but seemingly had to fire a shot or two in the process. The land, too, was strange, neither German nor Czech. The little towns near the border, with their houses linked by fences and their decorated arches over the gates, had the look of Slavic villages....This country was the disputed Sudetenland." (Charles B. MacDonald, *United States Army in World War II; The European Theater of Operations: The Last Offensive* [Washington: U.S. Army Center of Military History, 1951], 467.)

2. That Wagner was Hitler's favorite composer is coincidental here, but fitting in the context of the scenery. In fact, historians have termed this ending period of the Third Reich as precisely that: *Goetterdaemmerung.*

3. My physical features had radically changed in two months. When called to duty on March 16, I looked a little thinner in the face than the 1944 passport photo which accompanies this memoir, weighed about 55 kilograms (120 pounds), and stood about 162 centimeters (nearly 5-1/2 feet). Now I was gaunt, disheveled, and exhausted.

4. I wouldn't have risked this adventure a second time around; the consequences of getting caught could have been fatal.

5. Rationalizing the specter of this man is no diversion from descriptions of POW camp life. Rather, it shows how close sanity and insanity can become in a situation like ours, and illustrates deductively how Hitler wanted to be the savior, but ended up being the Satan. Symbolically, the German people fell for the lure of National Socialism in legitimately pursuing their own well-being as a nation, only to fall victim to an ideology they were mentally, politically, and spiritually not equipped to counter in time.

Also, this incident was the only time I remember seeing an American inside the stockade. For the rest of the time the Americans watched the spectacle of misery from the existentially safe distance outside the fence. Good and bad are not separated by clear lines like a fence, but rather the no-man's-land is shaded. Also, the American reader should understand the historical relationships between German church and state and its role in German nationalistic thinking and political life, and I think it interesting to see later in this chapter how German army chaplain Werthmann perceived the meaning of U.S. interrogation.

6. "*Bericht ueber die Internierung des Feldgeneralvikars Werthmann nach seinen Tagebuchaufzeichnungen* (Report about the Internment of Field General Vicar Werthmann after his Diary Entries)" in Michael Fischl, ed., *Die Amerikaner Kommen* (The Americans are Coming) (Tittling: Verlag Herbert Dorfmeister, 1995), 25–27 (translation H. Pfrengle's).

7. Ibid.

8. Indeed, the one major institution in Germany the Nazis could not break or weaken much was the Roman Catholic Church. It had survived more formidable foes than the Nazis. While waging war, Hitler could not afford to alienate the churches completely, and Nazi militancy against the major churches in the 1930s faded after war began. Strange (only to a simplistic mind) as it may seem to observers who might wonder why Hitler had not cracked down on organized religion—a potential obstructionist and thorn in his side—the answer is he needed the churches and their flocks in pursuing his goals.

9. Ibid.

10. Ibid., 12.

11. Ibid., 65.

12. Many years later, in my dealings with U.S. military matters, I had the occasion to see "responsibilities" neatly spelled out in mission statements, etc. But I often wondered about the essence of these prescriptive formulations when applied to contingencies or emergencies. In any event, our POW situation had formally annihilated any previously established leadership basis for responsibility. But then I derived my feeling of responsibility from the trust my comrades placed in me, and the role as a leader back home, a role which seemed to have held under our combat exposure since, and our captivity now.

13. The POW camp at Tittling was about 600 kilometers (about 390 miles) as the crow flies east of our home. We were probably the first POWs to get discharged from Tittling. Less than a year later, the camp was dissolved, and some POWs were handed over to the nearby Russians, according to hearsay documented in local eyewitness accounts.

14. Bathing—a luxury indeed! I remember having taken my last "bath" in a cold Boehmerwald stream about two days before our capture, over three weeks without washing. The last real bath, a shower, was at the school in Selb in the third week of April, and the next one was at Straubing in early June, where my life became more civilized again.

CHAPTER 7

1. The U.S. purpose was twofold: to get liberated DPs, some of them marauding the German countryside, under control, and put them to work as guards or at military construction sites. I heard of incidents where these guards had to be guarded by the Americans to prevent looting. In hindsight, the DPs' life was not bad in view of the considerable financial assistance the German government later gave the DPs to settle there.

2. Later I gave one of the maps to a friend who had fought in Rommel's *Afrikakorps* and was taken prisoner in Tunisia. He ended up in a POW camp in Nebraska where, in his own words, he had the best time of the whole war.

3. We did stay in touch for many years. Xaver's business was booming, and after I became a student of architecture, I provided my design inputs into the model for a new house he was planning.

CHAPTER 8

1. Coincidentally, the last part of this sentence could allegorically paraphrase the feelings of many Germans about the War Crimes Tribunal held later in that city, with the added psychological challenge of not leaving the lessons learned from Nuremberg behind.

2. Hans and I communicated with each other for years until losing track. He became a college teacher and was active in politics in the Darmstadt area.

EPILOGUE

1. Here, in a situation of great personal want, existentially refers to a condition where the mind becomes geared to preserving a minimum of life's awareness and existence as a human being vice a vegetable. The inner self and physical existence seem to merge. This reflects aspects of views by the 20th-century European philosophers Heidegger and Sartre of man and being.

2. Stephen Mufson, "Mao and Later: A Taste of History," in *Washington Post*, May 16, 1996.

3. Helmut Ritgen, "The Demand that Dragged the War On," in *Statesman*, New Delhi, as quoted from the article's German translation, June 18, 1995.

4. Interestingly, and somewhat ironically, 52 years later the German parliament passed a law that rehabilitates former *Wehrmacht* members who had been sentenced by the *Wehrmacht* military justice system for desertion. The law finds that their sentencing had been unlawful by the standards of a constitutional state, and awards each such survivor a one-time compensation payment of DM 7,500 (see German Information Center, "Deutschland Nachrichten," New York: 23 May 1997, 7).

5. Percy E. Schramm, ed., *Kriegstagebuch des Oberkommando der Wehrmacht* IV (War Diary of the *Wehrmacht*'s Supreme Command) (Frankfurt/Main: 1965), 1281 (translation H. Pfrengle's).

Glossary

The following primarily German names, abbreviations, and terms are used in this book. German usage is italicized.

Afrikakorps: (Rommel's) Africa Corps

Anschluss: The 1938 unification of Germany and Austria, orchestrated by Hitler

Artillerie: Artillery

Atlantikwall: Atlantic Coastal defenses in France and Belgium

Blitzkrieg: "Lightning" war .

Bund Deutscher Maedel: Federation of German Maidens

der/die/das: the

Deutsch(e): German(s)

Deutschland: Germany

Dorf: Village

Dreilaendereck: Point where borders of Germany, Luxembourg, and France meet

Eisenbahn-Baukompanie: Railroad construction company in Army Engineer Corps

Endsieg: Final victory

Ersatzkaffee: Replacement, imitation coffee

Faehnleinfuehrer: *Jungvolk* leader in charge of about 100–150 boys

Feldgendarmerie: Military police

Flak: Anti-aircraft gun or system (*Fliegerabwehrkanone*)

Flakhelfer: *Flak* helper (16-year-old high-school student drafted to man *Flak*)

Flusspioniere: River engineers

Frontbegradigung(en): Retrograde or readjustment of front line(s) (really meaning "retreat")

Fuehrer: Leader

Gauleiter: Nazi state governor

Generaloberst: Colonel general

Gestapo: Secret State Police (*Geheime Staatpolizei*)

Goetterdaemmerung: "Twilight of the Gods" (Wagner opera)

Goldfasan: Gold pheasant, nickname for Nazi official

Hauptjungzugfuehrer: No. 2 *Jungvolk* leader in charge of about 100–150 boys

Heer: Army

Heeresgruppe: Army group

Heil Hitler: Hail Hitler (salute)

Heimat: Homeland

Heimatheer: Army units stationed on German soil (effective September 1944)

Hitlerjugend: Hitler Youth

Hoehe(n): Hill(s)

Jungenschaftsfuehrer: *Jungvolk* leader in charge of about 10–12 boys

Jungmaedelbund: Federation of Young Maidens

Jungstammfuehrer: *Jungvolk* leader in charge of about 600 boys

Jungvolk: Young people, 10–14-year-old class of Youths

Jungzugfuehrer: *Jungvolk leader* in charge of about 30–40 boys

K.P.: (U.S.) Kitchen police/duty

Kaffeeklatsch(e): Coffee gossip session(s)

Kameradendiebstahl: Stealing from comrades

Kommissbrot: Soldier's staple bread field ration

Krieg: War

Kumpels: Buddies

Lebensraum: Living space

Leibstandarde Adolf Hitler: Hitler's elite SS Guard Regiment

Luftwaffe: Air Force

Marine-Seesportschule: Navy sports training school

Marschbefehl: Marching or moving orders to a unit or individual

Mein Kampf: Hitler's autobiography

Messerschmitt: Aircraft manufacturer, type of aircraft

Nazi: Short for National Socialist German Workers Party (*Nationalsozialistische Deutsche Arbeiterpartei): NSDAP*

OKH: Army High Command *(Oberkommando des Heeres)*

OKW: High Command of the Armed Forces (*Oberkommando der Wehrmacht*)

Panzer: Tank, armored

Panzerfaust: Single-shot, shaped-charge antitank weapon

Panzergruppe: Panzer forces group, armored group

Panzervernichtungs-Brigade: Tank destruction brigade

Realgymnasium: Approximate educational equivalent of a combination of American high school and junior college, with academic emphasis on natural science, mathematics, and three mandatory foreign languages

Reich: Commonwealth; periods of German history: First Reich, Holy Roman Empire to 1806; Second Reich, Bismarck's reign, 1871–90; Third (*Drittes) Reich*, Hitler's "Thousand-Year Reich," 1933 to May 8, 1945

Reichsarbeitsdienst: Reich Labor Service

Reichsmarschall: Marshal of the Third Reich [Goering]

Reichsluftfahrtministerium: Reich Aviation Ministry

Reichspropagandaminister: Propaganda minister of the Third Reich [Goebbels]

Reichsverteidigungskommissar: Reich Defense Commissioner

Rittergut: Huge manor/farm combination dating back to the age of Prussian landed aristocracy

SA: Storm trooper (*Sturmabteilung*), "Brownshirts"

Savoir vivre: (French) lavish lifestyle ("knowing how to live well")

Schlacht: (Literally) slaughter, battle

SD: SS intelligence service (*Sicherheitsdienst*)

Sieg Heil!: Hail victory!

S.O.S.: (U.S.) "same old shit"

SS: Nazi elite guard, protecting squad (*Schutzstaffel*)

Sondermeldung(en): Special radio report(s)

Strausswirtschaft(en): Rural inn(s)

Stunde Null: Zero hour, day "one"

Sturmgewehr 44: Automatic assault rifle Model 1944

Sudetendeutsche: Ethnic German population of Czechoslovakia

Unterbannfuehrer: Jungvolk leader in charge of about 2,000 boys

V-2: Supersonic rocket

Vaterland: Fatherland, Germany

Verboten: Forbidden

Volkslieder: Folk songs

Volksmaske: People's (gas) mask

Volkssturm: People's (storm) home defense militia

Waffen-SS: Military arm of the Nazi Party

Wald: Woods, forest

Wehrmacht: German armed forces

Wehrmachtsbericht(e): Armed Forces Report(s), selected military news brief(s)

Westwall: Siegfried (defense) Line in western Germany

Westwall-Ehrenzeichen: Medal ribbon for service on the Siegfried Line

Winterhilfswerk: Wintertime charity drive for needy civilians

Wunderwaffen: Miracle weapons

Wurst: Sausage

Bibliography

Books

Allen, Peter. *One More River: The Rhine Crossings of 1945*. New York: Barnes & Noble, 1990.

Arbeitsgruppe Lokalgeschichte. *Budenheim im Dritten Reich*. Budenheim, Ger.: 1985.

Bittere Zeit, NS Terror—Kriegsende—Wiederbeginn im Landkreis Tirschenreuth [book translation]. Pressath, Ger.: Buchhandlung Eckhard Bodner, 1995.

Brandenburg, Hans-Christian. *Die Geschichte der Hitlerjugend* [Second Edition]. Koeln, Ger.: Berend von Nottbeck, 1982.

Davis, Franklin M., Jr. *Across the Rhine*. Richmond, Va.: Time-Life Books, 1999.

Dear, I. C. B., and M. R. D. Foot, eds. *The Oxford Companion to World War II*. New York: Oxford University Press, 1995.

First United States Army: Report of Operations, 1 August 1944–22 February 1945 [undated, official U.S. Government publication].

Fischer, Ria. *Babenhausen als Garnisonsstadt*. Babenhausen, Ger.: Heimat- und Geschichtsverein Babenhausen e. V., 1991.

Fischl, Michael, ed. [book translation], *Die Amerikaner kommen: Frühjahr 1945; Archiv für das Dreiburgenland Heft 6*. Tittling, Ger.: Verlag Herbert Dorfmeister, 1995.

Griess, Thomas E., ed. *Atlas for the Second World War: Europe and the Mediterranean*. Wayne, N.J.: Avery Publishing Group, The West Point Military History Series, n.d.

Herbst, Jurgen. *Requiem For A German Past: A Boyhood Among the Nazis*. Madison: University of Wisconsin Press, 1999.

Heyes, Eileen. *Children of the Swastika*. Brookfield, Conn.: The Millbrook Press, 1993.

Keegan, John, ed. *Atlas of the Second World War*. London: Geographia, 1996.

Knopp, Guido. *Hitlers Kinder [Hitlers Children]*. Guetersloh, Ger.: C. Bertelsmann Verlag, 2000.

Koch, H. W. *The Hitler Youth: Origins and Development 1922– 1945*. New York: Barnes & Noble, 1996.

MacDonald, Charles B. *United States Army in World War II; The European Theater of Operations: The Last Offensive*. Washington: U.S. Army Center of Military, 1951.

Mondey, David. *Axis Aircraft of World War II*. London: Chancellor Press, 1996.

Ritgen, Helmut. *Die Geschichte der Panzer Lehr Division: Im Westen 1944–1945*. Stuttgart, Ger.: Motorbuch Verlag, 1979.

————. *Westfront 1944 Remembered: From Normandy to the Ardennes*. Winnipeg: J. J. Fedorowicz Publishing, 1995.

Schramm, Percy E., ed. [book translation], *Kriegstagebuch des Oberkommando der Wehrmacht* IV. Frankfurt/Main, Ger.: Suhrkamp, 1965.

Stein, R. Conrad. *World at War: Hitler Youth*. Chicago: Children's Press, 1985.

Whiting, Charles. *Siegfried: The Nazis Last Stand*. New York: Stein & Day, 1982.

Williamson, Gordon. *Loyalty is My Honor: Personal Accounts from the Waffen-SS*. Osceola, Wisc.: Motorbooks International, 1995.

Periodicals and Official Reports

German Information Center. "Deutschland Nachrichten," New York: 23 May 1997.

Hossfeld, Adolf [article translation]. "The Collapse in April 1945 in Sonneberg," in *Neue Presse*, January 30, 1993.

Mainzer Journal, August 25 and December 20, 1939.

Mufson, Stephen. "Mao and Later: A Taste of History," in *Washington Post*, May 16, 1996.

Munzel, Generalmajor Oskar, MGFA, No. B-360 [report translation]. "Tank Training Combat Command Thuringia, 27 March to 5 April 1945."

Ritgen, Helmut [article translation]. "The Demand that Dragged the War on," in *Statesman*, New Delhi, June 18, 1995.

Sagan, Guenter [article translation]. "The Destruction of Hauswurz in 1945," in *Fuldaer Zeitung*, February 21, 1996.

Schneider, Peter. "Invisible Man," *Los Angeles Times* Book Review, 22 June 1997.

Index

175

—